# Extracting Reconciliatic

*Extracting Reconciliation* argues that reconciliation constitutes a critical contemporary mechanism through which colonialism is seeking to ensure continuing access to Indigenous lands and resources.

Making use of two historical case studies concerned with the intersection of resource extraction, Crown/Inuit relations, and waste legacies in Nunavut, Canada, the authors illuminate the mechanisms of colonial and neoliberal governance globally that promise reconciliation while delivering the status quo. Through Indigenous and non-Indigenous anticolonial and posthuman concepts and theories, the book engages with the inhuman politics of settler colonial extractivism and explores the socio-ethical social justice dimensions, political possibilities, and environmental implications of a much more challenging and accountable reckoning between (settler) colonialism and Indigenous land rights.

This book is of interest to students and scholars in gender studies, postcolonial studies, environmental studies, Indigenous studies, and politics.

**Myra J. Hird** (DPhil Oxford) is Professor, elected Fellow of the Royal Society of Canada, and Queen's National Scholar in the School of Environmental Studies, Queen's University, Canada. Professor Hird is Director of the research project Waste Flow and has published 12 books and over 80 articles and book chapters on a diversity of topics relating to waste and science studies.

**Hillary Predko** (MES Queen's) is a researcher, writer, and artist based in Ontario. Her research explores issues around the materiality of waste, climate change, and social justice. Her Masters of Environmental Studies research explored the waste politics of resource extraction in Nunavut and earned Social Sciences and Humanities Research Council of Canada funding.

# More Than Human Humanities

Recent titles in series:

**Extracting Reconciliation**
Indigenous Lands, (In)human Wastes, and Colonial Reckoning
*Myra J. Hird and Hillary Predko*

For more information about this series, please visit: www.routledge.com/
More-Than-Human-Humanities/book-series/MTHH

# Extracting Reconciliation

Indigenous Lands, (In)human Wastes, and Colonial Reckoning

**Myra J. Hird and Hillary Predko**

Routledge
Taylor & Francis Group

LONDON AND NEW YORK

First published 2024
by Routledge
4 Park Square, Milton Park, Abingdon, Oxon OX14 4RN

and by Routledge
605 Third Avenue, New York, NY 10158

*Routledge is an imprint of the Taylor & Francis Group, an informa business*

© 2024 Myra J. Hird and Hillary Predko

The right of Myra J. Hird and Hillary Predko to be identified as authors of this work has been asserted in accordance with sections 77 and 78 of the Copyright, Designs and Patents Act 1988.

*British Library Cataloguing-in-Publication Data*
A catalogue record for this book is available from the British Library

*Library of Congress Cataloging-in-Publication Data*
Names: Hird, Myra J., author. | Predko, Hillary, author.
Title: Extracting reconciliation : Indigenous lands, (in)human wastes, and colonial reckoning / Myra J. Hird and Hillary Predko.
Description: New York, NY : Routledge, 2024. | Series: More than human humanities ; 1 | Includes bibliographical references and index. |
Identifiers: LCCN 2023026724 (print) | LCCN 2023026725 (ebook) |
ISBN 9781032379081 (hardback) | ISBN 9781032379098 (paperback) |
ISBN 9781003342526 (ebook)
Subjects: LCSH: Reconciliation—Canada—Political aspects—Case studies. | Indigenous peoples—Land tenure—Canada—Case studies. | Colonization—History—Case studies. | Indigenous peoples—Canada—Government relations. | Canada—Politics and government.
Classification: LCC JZ5584.C26 H57 2024 (print) | LCC JZ5584.C26 (ebook) | DDC 305.897/071—dc23/eng/20230612
LC record available at https://lccn.loc.gov/2023026724
LC ebook record available at https://lccn.loc.gov/2023026725

ISBN: 978-1-032-37908-1 (hbk)
ISBN: 978-1-032-37909-8 (pbk)
ISBN: 978-1-003-34252-6 (ebk)

DOI: 10.4324/9781003342526

Typeset in Times New Roman
by codeMantra

# Contents

# Acknowledgements

Myra and Hillary thank Cecilia Åsberg and Marietta Radomska for proposing that we write this book, and for their encouragement and unwavering support throughout the process. Myra and Hillary also thank Eleanor Catchpole Simmons and Charlotte Taylor at Routledge for helping to get this manuscript through all of its stages. We also thank the authors, activists, and knowledge keepers we cite – and the many others who did not make it into this book – for their inspiration.

Parts of Myra J. Hird and Alexander Zahara (2017) 'The Arctic Wastes' in Grusin, R. (ed) *Anthropocene Feminism*. University of Minnesota Press, pp.121–145 are reproduced in Chapter 4 and are used with the publisher and Alex's permissions. Parts of Chapter 4 are also adapted from an earlier version of Myra J. Hird, "Waste Legacies: Land, Waste, and Canada's DEW Line," *Northern Research* 42 (2016), 173–95 and used with the publisher's permission. Parts of Myra J. Hird, Hillary Predko and Micky Renders (2022) 'Decolonizing Posthumanism' in Grech, M. (ed) *Palgrave Handbook of Critical Posthumanism*. Palgrave Mamillan, pp. 1–20 are reproduced in Chapters 1 and Conclusions and are used with the publisher and Micky's permissions.

Myra thanks Hillary for the energetic discussions and pleasure in writing together, which has produced as much a friendship as a book. Myra dedicates this book to Inis, Eshe, and Christophe.

Hillary thanks Dr. Laura Jean Cameron and Dr. Amanda White, for their conversations and guidance as committee members, and Daemon Baliski, M.R. Sauter, Alex Leitch, and Lee Wilkins for their unending support. Thanks also to Myra for years of mentorship, collaborations, and walks throughout Montreal.

# Figure

# Introduction

## Anxious, soothing repetition

At the 2009 G20 Summit, Stephen Harper, former Canadian Prime Minister, made the claim that Canada is not, and never was, a colonial nation. Specifically, he stated: "We also have no history of colonialism" (Assembly of First Nations of Québec and Labrador, 2009). Harper made this claim after the federal government was legally obligated by an agreement between the Association of First Nations (AFN) and the former Canadian government, to apologize for the residential school system in Canada (Assembly of First Nations of Québec and Labrador, 2009: np). Twelve years later, in July 2021, non-Indigenous Canadians were shocked by the news that 215 unmarked graves were found on the grounds of a former residential school in Kamloops, British Columbia (*ABC News*, 2021: np). While initially, some pundits tried to cast this as a fake news story (Kennedy, 2022), the horrific truth – what Indigenous people have been telling Canadians for generations – began to emerge, as more unmarked graves continue to be found on residential school sites across Canada. Indeed, the Truth and Reconciliation Commission's (TRC) 2015 *Register of Confirmed Deaths of Named Residential School Students* and the *Register of Confirmed Deaths of Unnamed Residential School Students* had already laid bare the reality:

Canada's residential schools and residences for Aboriginal children operated for approximately 130 years.... The Commission has identified 3,200 deaths. For just under one-half of these deaths (49%), the government and the schools did not record the cause of death.... With a warrant, one could enter - by force, if need be - any house, building or place named in the warrant and remove the child.... Distressed, neglected, and abused, some students killed themselves. Poorly built and maintained buildings were fire traps.... As late as 1942, the principal of a residential school in Saskatchewan was unaware of any responsibility to report a death to provincial vital statistics officials.... Between 1936 and 1944, 200,000 Indian Affairs files were destroyed.... Many, if not most, of the several thousand children who died in residential schools are likely to be buried in unmarked and

DOI: 10.4324/9781003342526-1

untended graves.... Subjected to institutionalized child neglect in life, they
have been dishonored in death.

(Truth and Reconciliation Commission of Canada, 2015: 1–138)

The discovery of an increasing number of unmarked graves put more pressure
on Pope Francis and the Catholic Church to apologize for the sexual, physical,
and psychological abuses that took place in these 'schools' (what some Indigenous peoples call prisons or forced labour camps), over generations. In 2022,
Pope Francis visited Canada, toured a number of Indigenous communities,
and met with residential school survivors. He publicly apologized on behalf
of his Church. On his flight back to the Vatican, the Pope was asked why he
didn't use the term 'cultural genocide' as the TRC had done in its 2015 report,
to which he replied, "It's true, I didn't use the word because it didn't come to
my mind" (in Chambraud, 2022: np). This response hit the headlines. Buried
deeper in the news was this: "Canada agreed to 'forever discharge' Catholic
entities from their promise to raise $25 million for residential school survivors
and also picked up their legal bill...." (Taylor, 2022: np).

Around the same time that the TRC reports were made public (and free
to download for people with access to the internet), Justin Trudeau's Liberal
government was engaged in a tense race to win the 2015 federal election, and
wrest the country's reins from Conservative Prime Minister Stephen Harper
and his nine-year leadership. Headlines such as "Liberals call for full implementation of Truth and Reconciliation Commission recommendations"
were common (*Liberal Party of Canada*, 2015: np). At the time, Trudeau was
unequivocal:

> On behalf of the Liberal Party of Canada and our Parliamentary Caucus,
> I affirm our unwavering support for the TRC's recommendations, and
> call on the Government of Canada to take immediate action to implement
> them. As leaders and legislators, we have a responsibility to act. The truth
> of what occurred has been established. Now we must all commit to the
> important work of reconciliation going forward.
>
> (Justin Trudeau, *Liberal Party of Canada*, 2015: np)

And yet, once in power, as well as paying the legal bills for the Catholic
Church to not pay the $25 million it had committed to residential school sur-
vivors, Prime Minister Trudeau "spent nearly $100M fighting First Nations in
court during his first years in power" (Forester, 2020: np).

In the next election cycle, Trudeau repeated his commitment to reconciliation and justice for Indigenous communities. After winning the 2019 general election, he reassured Canadians that "Reconciliation 'isn't just a word'"
(*APTN National News*, 2019: np). But in 2020, the Wet'suwet'en Nation and
the British Comumbian (BC) government clashed over Kinder Morgan's (a
multinational pipeline company) plans to construct and operate the Coastal

GasLink pipeline on Wet'suwet'en Nation territory. As the Wet'suwet'en Nation points out, this conflict is only the latest in a consistent and persistent struggle of this Nation to assert its rights since settler colonization began. In 2019, the BC government issued this statement on the reconciliation process between the Province and Office of the Wet'suwet'en:

> The Office of the Wet'suwet'en and Province of British Columbia are committed to explore a path forward together, government-to-government, that seeks to build trust over time and meaningfully advance reconciliation. This process has emerged from decades of denial of Wet'suwet'en rights and title. Both parties believe that the time has come to engage in meaningful nation-to-nation discussions with the goal of B.C. affirming Wet'suwet'en rights and title.
>
> (BC Gov News, Feb. 7, 2019: np)

Just one year after the statement on reconciliation was made, Wet'suwet'en land was aggressively invaded by the Royal Canadian Mounted Police (RCMP). Bruce McIvor, a lawyer representing the Wet'suwet'en Nation stated:

> Yesterday my Wet'suwet'en clients in northern British Columbia again faced the reality of what it too often means to be an Indigenous person in Canada. While Wet'suwet'en Hereditary Chiefs and their supporters seek to defend their land against a multinational pipeline company and a provincial government that appears to believe reconciliation occurs at the end of a gun, the RCMP again amassed an armed force in an attempt to overwhelm and subdue them…In preparation for a similar military-style raid against my clients last year, the RCMP employed a strategy of 'lethal overwatch' and using as much violence as they deemed necessary to 'sterilize the site'…This time around the RCMP assured Canadians that the police officers tasked with dismantling Wet'suwet'en camps, handcuffing unarmed land protectors and marching them off to jail had first undergone cultural awareness training.
>
> (*First People's Law*, Feb. 7, 2020: np)

Like so many interactions between Indigenous nations and communities and the various levels of the Canadian government, the Indigenous refusal to accede to increased government and industry-owned and controlled resource extraction, production, and distribution, the "path forward" proceeded to armed conflict. Even from governments that publicly commit to reconciliation as a goal, violence is part of the state's toolkit, warranted in the name of public safety. In 2019, Natural Resources Minister Jim Carr justified the deployment of Canada's military to disband a pipeline protest by publicly stating, "If people choose for their own reasons not to be peaceful, then the government of Canada, through its defence forces, through its police forces, will ensure that people will be kept safe" (in Lukacs, 2019: 96). With Coastal Salish and other Indigenous nations and communities throughout Canada supporting the Wet'suwet'en, as well as increasing numbers of non-Indigenous Canadians joining the protest and otherwise supporting the Nation against increased industrial resource extraction, the Canadian news read, "'Reconciliation is dead and we will shut down Canada,' Wet'suwet'en supporters say" (in Alex Ballingall for *Toronto Star,* Feb. 13, 2020).

Land and the resources above and below its surface remain at the centre of these conflicts, and current reconciliation policies clumsily try to smooth over the cracks of a crumbling settler colonial foundation. At the Our Land, Our Future national summit, in November 2017 a young woman named Rosalie LaBillois responded to SNC-Lavalin Vice-President's question, "What is the good life to you?" by saying:

> The connection that we have to land, no one should be able to take that away. We need to live our truths when we make decisions about resource development. The government has tried to tell us who we are. We are so much more than they think.
>
> (in Lukas, 2022: np)

## Introduction

We (Hillary, born in Canada to parents descended from British and Ukrainian settlers; and Myra, born in Canada to British settlers) are White cis women settler Canadians.[1] We met through a formal relationship (graduate student; supervisor) structured by a tertiary institution (Queen's University) that was founded on, and continues to occupy, unceded Anishinaabe Nation and Haudenosaunee Nation territories belonging to the First Nations of the Confederation of First Fires and the Haudenosaunee Confederacy. If you email either of us, you'll see that we have Indigenous Land Acknowledgment statements. Queen's University, like other universities across Canada, was recently embroiled in a controversy concerned with academics falsely claiming Indigenous identity. According to our institution's website, "The Office of Indigenous Initiatives builds community, advances reconciliation/conciliation and integrates Indigenous ways of knowing and being into the fabric and life of the university" (2023: np). In 2021, a 53-page anonymous report that included certified copies of documents, such as census data and marriage certificates, accused four Queen's University faculty of Indigenous identity theft, claiming to be Indigenous rather than actually being Indigenous (Flaherty, 2021: np). Apparently blindsided, Queen's University spokesperson Mark Erdman responded to the report by publicly stating, "We reject the anonymous document in question, which is misleading and contains factual inaccuracies including some genealogical information of individuals named in the document" (in Chin and Williams, 2021: np).

Queen's University is by no means the only tertiary institution accused of hiring and retaining what have come to be known as Pretendians. As Melissa Ridgen defines the term,

> Pretendians – noun – A person who falsely claims to have Indigenous ancestry – meaning it's people who fake an Indigenous identity or dig up an old ancestor from hundreds of years ago to proclaim themselves as Indigenous today. They take up a lot of space and income from First Nation, Inuit and Metis Peoples.
>
> (Ridgen, 2021: np)

The institution's initial response to not even consider the accusations sparked a proverbial fire. Indigenous academics across Canada and the United States signed an open letter calling on Queen's to retract its statement, and to open an investigation. As Pam Palmater, Chair in Indigenous Governance at Ryerson University, commented, "Queen's response is really concerning…. It was done so quickly," she said. "It appears to be a knee-jerk reaction, and it was done without consultation with the First Nations that it impacts or with the wider Indigenous faculty and staff and students at Queen's University" (in Chin and Pfeffer, 2021: np). The open letter reads in part:

> Queen's University did what perhaps most settler-colonial institutions would do. They doubled down, ignored troubling information about several of their employees, issuing a statement before coordinating any meaningful dialogue with all of the Indigenous faculty and staff at Queen's and with people within Indigenous communities. It is unacceptable for universities to simply use an honour system when it comes to verifying the legitimacy of claims made by any faculty, staff or student claiming to be Indigenous.
>
> (ibid)

Facing negative press and increasing pressure, Queen's Chancellor, the Right Honourable Murray Sinclair, chaired Queen's own mini-version of the Truth and Reconciliation investigation (First Peoples Group, 2022) into how Queen's should best respond to this situation. Murray Sinclair was well-equipped for this task, having chaired Canada's Truth and Reconciliation Commission. When the task force concluded its work and issued its report, the University issued a public statement stating that it accepted the report's recommendations. In the aftermath of this, and other Pretendian controversies across Canada, Kim Tallbear had this to say: "I wouldn't be surprised if 25% of the people identifying as Indigenous for hiring in Canada are not" (in Leo, 2022: np).

Ambitious politicians and educational institutions are neither isolated nor distinct examples: they are part of a pattern called reconciliation. This is a short book, so let's get straight to the point. Canada,[2] like the United States, Nouvelle

Calédonie, New Zealand, South Africa and other places (land, water, air) where colonizers settled, is focused on reconciliation. In Canada, reconciliation – as noun (the state of having regained respectful relationship), verb (acts of), rhetorical technique (witness my commitment!), bargaining tool (Nunavut's Land Claims Agreement), Judeo-Christian rooted commandment (honour thy parents, no matter how gravely they have abused and traumatized you), symbol (of good relations), mantra for mantra's sake, capital (Every Child Matters Orange T-Shirts on sale at Amazon.ca), and much more – is persistently and enthusiastically repeated in tweets, Facebook posts, newspaper articles, political speeches, and industry promotional videos.[3] The Canadian federal government (known as the 'Crown') repeats – in House of Commons speeches, interviews, White Papers, and so on – its commitment to reconciliation. We may trace this push to reconciliation to the 1990 'Oka crisis', when the municipality of Oka approved a golf course expansion on unceded traditional territory of the Kanien'kéha:ka (Mohawk) of Kanehsatà:ke. After trying every means possible to protect their land, from the seventeenth century onwards, Mohawks staged a 78-day blockade and protest that the Crown ended through military force.

In the messy public relations aftermath, the federal government launched the Royal Commission on Aboriginal Peoples in 1991, ostensibly designed to improve Indigenous-Crown relations. The report found that the struggles Indigenous communities face were all underpinned by land, air, and water dispossession, yet government funding was allocated to programs that target individuals (Lukacs, 2019: 140). This is not a one-off response: it's a trend, repeated, for instance, in the aftermath of the 2015 Truth and Reconciliation Commission. While the report itself details the importance of land, policy response stresses "the injury done to individuals instead of injury done to nations" (ibid: 141). As Sean Carleton notes:

> Trudeau was elected [in 2015], in part, on a platform of reconciliation and improving relations with Indigenous peoples. Though apologies, financial compensation and renaming government buildings are important steps in the right direction, *meaningful reconciliation in Canada also requires the return of stolen land.*
>
> (2021: np, emphasis added)

And here lies the rub. Our first argument is that Canada's settler/colonial neoliberal capitalist system purposefully deploys reconciliation as an ideological, structural, and procedural tool to secure *increased* access *to*, and *control over*, Indigenous lands and waters for resource extraction. We use the bulky term 'settler/colonial neoliberal capitalism' purposefully. Throughout the book, we adopt Lorenzo Veracini's distinction between colonialism and settler colonialism thus: "whereas colonialism reinforces the distinction between colony and metropole, settler colonialism erases it" (2011: 3; see also Veracini, 2010). This erasure is important in the Canadian context. It allows, for example, the Crown to build up military operations in Nunavut and on other Indigenous lands and waters in the name of 'national security' for "all Canadians" (Government of Canada, 2014: np). It forefronts the Crown's intimate relationship with resource extraction industries to the "benefit of all Canadians" (ibid). As such, settler/colonial neoliberal capitalism affords an attenuation to resource exploration and extraction and sheds light on "what settler colonialism continually denies – its own existence and the deeply violent geographies that sustain it" (Cameron, 2015: 20).

We refer to neoliberalism as those government policies that reflect and encourage free trade, globalization, deregulation, privatization, the private sector, and individualization in the economy and society. The Crown's land and water negotiations with Indigenous communities are predicated on a profound yet subtle shift to individual rather than community rights (see Howard-Wagner, Bargh, and Atamirano-Jiménez, 2018; Atamirano-Jiménez, 2014; MacDonald, 2011). Witness, for instance, former Prime Minister Stephen Harper's First Nations Property Ownership Initiative, whereby reserve land would be converted to individual private property. As Preston observes, "That neoliberalism figures individual private property as a fundamental and necessary element of human progress inevitably leads, within the structure of settler colonialism, to an attack on collective rights and Indigenous Self-determination" (2013: 49). This, as we will demonstrate, includes not only private property rights but extends to resource extraction's aftermath, contaminating and toxic waste. And we refer to capitalism as the world's hegemonic political and economic organization to, always and in all circumstances, maximize private profit.[4] Capitalism explains how and why Tim Hortons, Canadians' unofficial coffee supplier, sells reconciliation donuts to customers: "Tim Hortons' Orange-Sprinkled Fundraising Donut is Back in Support of Indigenous Charities" (*ToDoCanada*, 2022, np). Commenting on the donut sold on Indigenous Reconciliation Day, Tanya Tagaq pointedly wrote on her Twitter feed, "Get me the Native trauma donut" (2022, np). However bulky, using the term settler/colonial neoliberal capitalism is critical because it is the *convergence* of these distinct structures, forces, policies, and practices – that explains reconciliation's terms and implementation.

Resource extraction and its capital profits (with their global security and sovereignty implications) are, we argue, at the heart of the Crown and resource extraction industry's chorus for reconciliation. Reconciliation, in other words, is synonymous with *increased settler/colonial neoliberal capitalism*. As such, we want to be clear that the aim of our critique is not to 'do' reconciliation better. Or reconcile more. Or less. Each would be to add power to the well-worn promises that the Crown and industry make to Indigenous communities for more jobs, (colonial) education, (functioning) facilities, potable water, health care, and so on – an array of promises whose sum amounts to greater assimilation into settler/colonial neoliberal capitalism: a technique deployed, over and over again, from the Gradual Civilization Act (1857), Treaties 1 through 11, the Indian Act and all of its Amendments, to the Indian Advancement Act.

Embedded in the settler colonial imagination of sovereignty is the messy juxtaposition of the Arctic as simultaneously (1) the "True North strong and free" — a remote and pristine landscape whose innocent history embodies an aesthetic of uncontained and uncontaminated wilderness; (2) the North as Canada's largest and most diverse emerging resource for industrial extraction and a vital piece of the circumpolar pie, and increasingly (3) the North as anthropogenic trace and therefore "a symbolic pinnacle for global sustainable development" (Hird, 2021). The dramatic increase in demand for northern natural resources over the past 20 years has only intensified with the prospect of climate change making these resources more accessible. According to Crown-Indigenous Relations and Northern Affairs Canada, the North contains approximately 25% of Canada's remaining discovered recoverable crude oil and natural gas and approximately 40% of Canada's projected future discoveries. This means more people and equipment moving temporarily from South to North, much more drilling and extraction, and, inevitably, more waste (ibid). As we write this book, the office of Ontario Mines Minister George Pirie held a press conference in which he stated that the Ring of Fire[5] may be worth a trillion dollars in profits (Turner, 2023).

It is within this ongoing settler colonial neoliberal capitalist context that we are researching waste issues in Nunavut. Through funding from the federal Canadian government, our research is not intended to raise Inuits' awareness of waste issues in their territory – Inuit are very aware of the legacy industrial and military waste littering their territory as well as the waste burdens they sustain from ever-increasing industrial, military, and retail enterprises (see, for example, Boutet, 2014). Our main objective is to raise settler Canadian awareness about these issues as a necessary precursor to taking responsibility for this waste, as part of a much larger settler colonial 'reckoning'. As Jeannette Armstrong succinctly challenges "[I]magine interpreting for us your own people's thinking toward us, instead of interpreting for us, our thinking, our lives, our stories" (in Regan, 2010: 235). This book is our attempt to do just this; our aspirational audience are non-Indigenous people who have settled on, or otherwise profit from, colonized Indigenous lands.[6]

Our second argument relates to the first. In this book, we argue that there is a settler/colonial neoliberal capitalist intellectual trend to extract – as resource – Indigenous ideas, concepts, and knowledge (Watts, 2013; Todd, 2016), in the name of *contributing to reconciliation*. This, we argue, amounts to a *dual extraction* of Indigenous lands and Indigenous knowledge in the service of settler/colonial ambitions. As such, we question whether, and if so then how, it is possible to ethically engage with Indigenous knowledges *as settlers* within colonial structures (universities) and systems (Western education), by forefronting Indigenous knowledge without seeking to 'weave', 'blend', 'intertwine', 'integrate' or otherwise render Indigenous ontologies and epistemologies compatible with, or palatable to, Western hegemonic ideologies (Wilson, 2008, Tuck and Yang, 2012). Rather than grapple with this tension, some settlers have instead made disingenuous and harmful claims that they are themselves Indigenous – an insidious example of knowledge extraction and a settler move to innocence (Tuck and Yang, 2012).

Chapter 1 provides a critical analysis of the major arguments used to support reconciliation between Indigenous peoples and settler colonial states. Drawing on Indigenous, anti-colonial, and posthuman concepts and theories, this chapter examines the incommensurability of settler and Indigenous ontologies and epistemologies, arguing that attempts to reconcile these differences through 'addition', 'incorporation', or other strategies actually reinforces, rather than meaningfully reconciles, differential power relations between settler/colonial neoliberal capitalist and Indigenous knowledge systems.

The next two chapters offer short case studies to illustrate the foundational problems with reconciliation. Chapter 2 examines the history of the Geological Survey of Canada's exploration of the Eastern Arctic, focusing particularly on the 1903–1904 survey conducted by A.P. Low. Expanding on Kathryn Yusoff's argument that "there is not geology on one hand and stories about geology on the other" (2018: 34), this chapter explores the critical role geological surveys played in settler colonial mining ambitions and pre-reconciliation dispossession tactics. As well as planting flags throughout the Arctic Archipelago to materially and symbolically establish Crown possession and sovereignty, the geological mapping survey also studied Inuit – their bodies, behaviours, nomadic patterns, and family relations in order to establish a colonial subject position in relation to settler geo-logics. Chapter 3 brings to the fore the reconciliation as dispossession at the heart of the post-1970 Comprehensive Land Claims Agreement policy. Through Hillary's knowledge creation methodology that includes an embroidered tapestry of the settlement area and map of Inuit-Owned-Land parcels, this chapter traces recent resource negotiations in the territory and critiques world-wide congratulatory rhetoric surrounding the Nunavut Land Claims Agreement as an example of successfully reconciling Indigenous sovereignty within settler-colonial governance.

Chapter 4 situates waste as a key material, rhetorical and symbolic manifestation of legacy and ongoing settler/colonial capitalism as well as contemporary neoliberal governance practices to argue that waste itself is a key part of the settler colonial context within which Indigenous peoples continue to live. Indeed, colonial powers have sought to align Indigenous peoples themselves *as waste* in a systematic program to render Indigenous people inhuman. As such, this chapter considers waste as the material and symbolic fallout of settler/colonial resource extraction development and the Western ideologies deployed to justify it.

The final chapter draws connections between reconciliation efforts and waste legacies, situating both within the ongoing project of settler/colonial resource extraction in Canada. We argue that these wastes leave behind indeterminate inheritances that require urgent ethical shifts in relationality and responsibility: in short, *a reckoning*. Chapter 5 traces how Indigenous knowledges, expertise, and land rights claims are precipitating a reckoning with colonial systems. The foundation of reckoning is Indigenous sovereignty of lands and waters, governance, histories, languages, educations, and cultures. The book concludes by bringing into sharp relief the speculative differences between reconciliation and reckoning.

*Extracting Reconciliation* emerged from many hours of revisited conversations, scouring Indigenous and non-Indigenous writing, interviews, social media posts, newspaper articles, live talks, and informal conversations. We provide, in greater detail, our methodological approaches in previous works (Hird, 2021, 2022; Predko, 2022).

## Meanwhile, *Nuluujaat*

On the northern part of Baffin Island, inland from the coast, a large outcrop of rock rises from the tundra (QIA, nd). The mountain *nuluujaat* (ᓄᓗᔮᑦ) guides Inuit crossing this island. The surrounding land and waters are home to abundant animal life – for thousands of years, families in North Baffin travel by qimmiq team, by foot, and by kayak to harvest caribou, seal, fish, walrus, narwhal, birds, and hare (Wachowich, 1994: 10), with *nuluujaat* on the horizon.

## Notes

1 In this book, we identify ourselves as White settlers, and have otherwise chosen not to note the background of other authors noted. For a different approach, see Liboiron (2021).
2 There are many names for this land. For example, the Arctic is ᓄᓇᕗᑦ, or Nunavut ("our land") to Inuit (a name which predates Nunavut as a political entity by thousands of years). Many Indigenous peoples call North America *Turtle Island,* to honor Sky Woman, Creator, and the turtle who grew the world on its back (Oneida Nation, nd). In this monograph, we call the land Canada to speak more precisely to the actions of the settler-colonial state.
3 See, for example, Canada's Nuclear Waste Management Organization's video on Indigenous Engagement for permanent storage of high-level radioactive waste on Indigenous lands. https://www.nwmo.ca/en/A-Safe-Approach/About-the-Project/Working-in-Partnership/Engaging-With-People/Indigenous-Engagement.
4 We adopt William Carroll and J.P. Sapinski's concept of 'settler-capitalist' society, which extends Marx's definition of capital not as a "thing, but as a social relation between persons, established by the instrumentality of things". Within these social relations, capital is a "self-expanding process… [which] begins when a capitalist invests money capital to purchase means of production (machinery, raw materials, etc.) and to hire workers. Money capital is thereby converted into productive capital, as workers are set to work, producing new commodities. As those goods and services find buyers, capital once again takes the form of money. But since the labor performed by workers has added new value, the capitalist now has more money capital than was advanced initially". And so on. See *Organizing the 1%: How Corporate Power Works* (2018: 3).
5 The Ring of Fire, taken from the Canadian singer Johnny Cash song of the same name, refers to some 5,000 kilometers of several First Nations lands in what Canada calls the James Bay Lowlands of northern Ontario.
6 Some people identify themselves as 'treaty people'.

# 1 Reconciling reconciliation

## Introduction

To distract the settler colonial public from the central question of land, rec-onciliation has been sold as a set of steps individuals can take – just add and stir the right words and actions and an undefined, repatriation-free future will emerge. This, as Chapter 4 details with regard to waste, is an iteration of neo-liberalism, whereby the public is convinced that meaningful societal change is possible through individual action alone. Michael Maniates (2001) refers to this as the "plant a tree, ride a bike, save the world" phenomenon. As such, reconciliation is the magic assemblage of individual Canadians buying and displaying orange T-shirts, taking reservation tours, adding land acknowledg-ments to their email signatures, and so on. The neoliberal mantra (individual change is sufficient) is synergistic with settler colonialism focused on holding onto Indigenous land already stolen, and ensuring that as much land as pos-sible is accessible to resource extraction.

In many universities across Canada, this has resulted in calls for the 'In-digenization of the Academy', which has resulted in an intellectual trend to extract Indigenous ideas, concepts, and knowledge (Watts, 2013; Todd, 2016) in the name of reconciliation. In this chapter, we critique trends within some natural science, social science, and humanities fields that seek to 'weave', 'blend', 'intertwine', or otherwise 'integrate' Indigenous ontologies and epis-temologies (Wilson, 2008).

## Reconciliation as policy

Beginning in the 1870s, an estimated 150,000 First Nations, Inuit, and Mé-tis children were forced to attend residential 'schools'. Part prison and part forced labour camp, they were designed to assimilate Indigenous children into settler society through religious indoctrination, and where physical and sexual abuse was rampant (Union of Ontario Indians, 2013: 2). Incredibly, the last residential school closed as recently as 1996. Duncan Campbell Scott, Deputy Minister of Indian Affairs in 1920, saw the prisons as a solution to "the Indian

DOI: 10.4324/9781003342526-2

Problem" and wanted to see the residential schools run "until there is not a single Indian in Canada that has not been absorbed into the body politic and there is no Indian question, and no Indian Department" (ibid.: 3). On the surface, contemporary reconciliation politics in Canada target this injustice. Through the Truth and Reconciliation Commission's (TRC) 2015 final report and associated recommendations, the government's purported aim is to reconcile the genocidal legacy of residential schools with a fuzzy feel-good reassuring future of *mutual recognition* and *cross-cultural understanding*. Dig deeper and things get murky – since 2015, the Justin Trudeau government has pursued "a legal war of attrition to contain, minimize or dismiss Indigenous rights" (Lukacs, 2019: 148) to the tune of $70 million spent on court fees in 2018 alone (ibid.: 149).

The Canadian government's reconciliation strategy clearly favours performance over substance. In 2021, Trudeau's government made September 30th a national holiday, *Truth and Reconciliation Day.* Billed as a day for reflection and action, Trudeau was spotted spending the holiday on a foreign beach vacation (Stephenson and Gilmore, 2021). Meanwhile, the government has failed to take action on the TRC recommendations that directly concern it. As of 2022, only 13 of the 94 Calls to Action have been completed (Yellowhead Institute, 2022). Thus, federal reconciliation politics aims to distract the settler public from larger questions about land ownership, resource development, and Indigenous sovereignty – behind the veneer of public apologies, reconciliation is deployed as a (settler) colonial tool.

The TRC was established following the 2006 Indian Residential School Settlement Agreement, the largest class action lawsuit in Canadian history. While the truth commission was meant to establish a framework for justice for residential school survivors, the directive is far from transformative

> There is an emerging and compelling desire to *put the events of the past behind us* so that we can work towards a stronger and healthier future. The truth telling and reconciliation process as part of an overall holistic and comprehensive response to the Indian Residential School legacy is a sincere indication and *acknowledgment* of the injustices and harms experienced by Aboriginal people and *the need for continued healing*. This is a profound commitment to establishing new relationships embedded in *mutual recognition* and respect that will forge a brighter future. The truth of our common experiences will help set our spirits free and pave the way to reconciliation.
>
> (Indian Residential Schools Settlement Agreement, 2006: 1, emphasis added)

The remit of the Commission stresses acknowledgment, healing, and leaving the past behind rather than reparations, repatriation of land, or any reckoning with the legacy of individual and state actors who caused harm. Because reconciliation in Canada has been promoted by the government, based on law rather than social movement, the government exerts considerable control over the messaging (Regan, 2010). This state-sanctioned approach stresses that *individuals* coming together can right a set of wrongs (wrongs situated firmly in the past), without threatening the structure of the current, or future, settler-colonial state (Coulthard, 2014: 22).

In this legalistic, past-focused, and individual-change-oriented brand of reconciliation, "there [are] several great unmentionables: land, resources, and power, and the sharing of any of it" (Lukacs, 2019: 137). This canny sleight of hand obscures the government's fundamental interest in land, and its commitment to solidifying the assertion of Crown sovereignty (McIvor, 2021). While holidays and platitudes make the news, the Crown's legalistic approach to reconciliation is "primarily concerned with reconciling Aboriginal and Crown land title" (Regan, 2010: 60). In effect, there are two parallel reconciliations that rarely converse with each other. The first is a settler move to comfort (Lowman and Barker, 2015, also see Tuck and Yang, 2012) promoting individual settlers *bearing witness* to Indigenous people's testimonies of past harm, with no evidence that hearing these stories motivates settlers to "undertake an active, ethical engagement with this past, one that might force new relations of solidarity with Indigenous communities in a collective struggle for a more just future" (Roger Simon in Regan, 2010: 46). The second, less publicly promoted, reconciliation is the reconciliation of Aboriginal and Crown land title – which results in modern-day dispossession and increased resource extraction (discussed at length in Chapter 3).

Both Indigenous and settler scholars have thoroughly critiqued the reconciliation process (see, for example, Coulthard, 2014; McIvor, 2021; Wente, 2021; Lowman and Barker, 2015; Regan, 2010), but the imperfect process *could* have a real impact on Indigenous people's lives – if the TRC's 94 Calls to Action (CTA) were implemented. For example, Calls to Actions 45, 46, 47, and 49 require governments and faith organizations to repudiate the *Doctrine of Discovery*, which would upend land laws in Canada. Set out in a series of Roman Papal decrees between the twelfth and fifteenth centuries, the Doctrine of Discovery claimed Christian domination upon "discovered" lands and peoples beyond what is now Europe (Newcomb, 2008). The Doctrine of Discovery "was the legal means by which Europeans claimed rights of sovereignty, property, and trade in regions they allegedly discovered during the age of expansion" (Reid, 2010: 338). Such claims are foundational to the formation of legal territory and continue to be recognized by international law (ibid.: 338). Literally, slavery, genocide, and land theft were policy.

The 1452 Bull, *Dum Diversas,* calls upon European Catholics to "invade, capture, vanquish, and subdue all Saracens, pagans, and other enemies of Christ, to put them in perpetual slavery, and to take away all their possessions and property" (in Newcomb, 2008: 84). In 1513, the Spanish monarchy added the *Requerimiento*, an addendum to *Dum Diversas*, to explain that the decree applied to peoples who had never heard of Christ – priests would read the document – in Latin – at the outskirts of Indigenous villages before conquistadors laid siege to them, killing their inhabitants (ibid.: 36). The slightly later 1493 decree, *Inter Caetera*, claimed the right of dominion and possession over any "lands not possessed by any Christian prince" (in Newcomb, 2008: 46) to any (White male Catholic) European who – yes – drove a flag into the desired ground (see Chapters 3 and 4). In 1577, for instance, Martin Frobisher claimed the Arctic archipelago in the name of this decree:

> marched through the Countrey with Ensigne displaied, so far as thought needfulle, and now and then heaped up stones on high mountaines, and other places, in token of possession, as likewise to signifie unto such as hereafter may chance to arrive there, that possession is taken in behalfe of some Prince, by those who first found out the countrey…
>
> (in Reid, 2010: 340)

According to the Doctrine of Discovery and all of its legislative and policy offspring, when Frobisher heaped some stones (the permafrost equivalent to driving a stick into the ground), he made a legal claim to land and water – a literal, legal, and symbolic act repeated over centuries throughout Africa, Asia, Australia, New Zealand, and the Americas (Newcomb, 2008). In Canada, the Doctrine of Discovery[1] underpins all land claim negotiations and land relations between Indigenous people and the Crown (Reid, 2010). Formal repudiation would call into question Crown control over lands that were never formally ceded. As such, Canadian governments "have responded with silence" (McIvor, 2021: 16) to these calls.

Even more straightforward CTAs remain unfulfilled. Calls to Actions 6 to 12 target "the colonial legacy of assimilative, violent, and chronically underfunded systems of education that Indigenous children and peoples experience in Canada" (Yellowhead Institute, 2022: 15), in an attempt to make amends for the legacy of destructive "education" at residential schools and its long shadow. Indigenous peoples experience systemic barriers to accessing (colonial) education, resulting in "lower rates of educational attainment, which is one contributor (among many) to higher unemployment rates, fewer employment opportunities, and lower incomes" (ibid.: 15). CTA 9 implores the federal government to prepare and publish annual reports comparing funding for Indigenous children on and off reserves, yet the government has only provided data for 2016–2017 before ceasing to update the website (ibid.: 15). CTA 11 calls for the government to provide adequate funding for First Nations students seeking post-secondary education. In 2021, the federal budget included $150.6 million over two years, for Indigenous post-secondary students – less than what had been allotted in previous budgets (CBC, 2022). The budget also detailed a ten-year funding mechanism to escalate education funding for Indigenous children to parity with funding for non-Indigenous children. But as educator Leslee White-Eye has noted, seeking funding parity today, after schools in Indigenous communities have been underfunded for generations, does not achieve equality, and certainly not equity (in Yellowhead Institute, 2022: 17). The numbers that don't appear in the budget are the legal fees Crown-Indigenous Relations and Northern Affairs Canada (CIRNAC) incur fighting Indigenous people in court – the department spent "$58 million on legal services [in 2020], two times more than the RCMP or Defence Department respectively and more than any federal department other than the Canada Revenue Agency" (APTN, 2020). Instead of taking real action on reconciliation promises it has made, the government of Canada takes Indigenous peoples to court to avoid financial responsibility. Meanwhile reconciliation rhetoric has set off a series of myopic trends in settler education.

## Awkward implementation

At a time when the impact of settler colonization is being examined – spurred on through events such as the release of Canada's *Truth and Reconciliation Commission Report* (2015), the ongoing Idle No More movement (2012) and the recent *Black Lives Matter* movement (2020) – universities throughout the old and new world are scrambling in the 'race to Indigenize'. Universities such as the University of Alberta and the University of Calgary have hired (self-identified) Indigenous faculty and added Indigenous courses and content. Others are renaming buildings and 'encouraging' faculty and staff to add acknowledgement statements to their email signatures. Yet, as Johnson et al. note:

> Universities and academic disciplines of science and social science have unequivocally been part of the structure and infrastructure of European colonial power and its specific impacts on particular Indigenous peoples and their places and institutions. Entry of Indigenous voices into both the academy and political institutions has been—and typically remains—contingent and conditional.
>
> (2016: 2)

As such, initiatives that 'add' Indigenous faculty, staff and students to a hegemonic (settler) colonial system do not guarantee more than a 'stir' effect. Neither can it be the expectation that these Indigenous academics bear the burden of transforming the system that oppresses them: the "lonely only" as Sefanit Habton puts it (2017: 1). As Jana-Rae Yerxa succinctly argues, "settler comfort cannot be a burden that Indigenous peoples must carry" (2014; see also Hunt, 2014; Rushmore, 2020). Indeed, these efforts contribute more to the kind of reconciliation noted above that focuses on individual responsibility and side-steps the requirements of decolonization, which include "the rematriation of land, the regeneration of relations, and the forwarding of Indigenous and Black and queer futures" (la paperson, 2017: 2). It is easier to acknowledge stolen land than to repatriate it, or even share its profits. Similarly, it is easier to selectively borrow, utilize, or blend Indigenous knowledges within Western knowledge systems than to take seriously the incommensurability of these ontologically separate and conflicting systems, and its implications.

## Decolonizing critical posthumanism

Posthumanism emerged from extended debates within philosophy, discourse studies, and other disciplines about the limits of humanism for thinking through urgent concerns, including planetary changes wrought by the Anthropocene. From Michel Foucault's Nietzsche-inspired 'death of Man' (1989 [1966]), to Jacques Derrida's 'ends of Man' (1969), to ruminations about the ethical treatment of nonhuman creatures, posthumanism takes seriously the question as to what human emerges – if any – after universal subjectivity. While their entry points differ, posthuman approaches are linked by a shared goal to expose the foundational principle that anchored Western philosophy – 'Man' – in order to critique, and, crucially, to imagine, humanity beyond humanism. This imperative, as Myra acerbically put it, is to "figure out ways to survive humanism" (2009: 133).

One route traces debates within humanism's philosophical legacy that championed Man as the measure of all things, and justified His exploitation of nature and the 'other'; an abject category herding together racialized, gendered, and other subaltern subjectivities (see, for instance, Fanon, 1963; Foucault, 1966; Braidotti, 2013; Irigaray, 1974/1985; Spivak, 1988). Posthumanism engages with longstanding critiques of the violence of these universalist ideals from Haitian revolutionaries fighting for Black peoples' rights (Fuertes, 2010) to Giorgio Agamben's post-Holocaust articulation of 'bare life' (1998). As such, one of the central organizing objectives of posthumanism is to open up alternative subject positions with sexualized, racialized, and naturalized differences offering alternative models of human subjectivity (Braidotti, 2013: 38).

Another route concentrates analyses beyond the (however loosely categorized) human species towards non- or inhuman life in efforts to critically challenge the neo-Darwinian hierarchy of species (Braidotti and Hlavajova, 2018; Hird, 2009). Other posthuman approaches turn on the ethical relationship between human and non-human animals (see for instance Singer, 1975; Haraway, 2003; Donaldson and Kymlika, 2011), arguing that animals deserve at minimum co-citizenship and, ultimately, sovereignty. Other posthuman approaches focus less on rights- or ethics-based arguments in favour of analyses of agency (see, for example, Deleuze and Guattari, 1987; Bennett, 2010). Karen Barad's agential realism, for instance, offers a "posthumanist formulation of performativity [that] makes evident the importance of taking account of 'human', 'nonhuman', and 'cyborgian' forms of agency" (2003: 826). Instead of considering agency as ontologically circumscribed to human subjects who enact their will on the world, this relational ontology considers phenomena, or dynamic entanglements of relationalities where agency is enacted through ongoing reconfigurations (Barad, 2003: 818). If agency is doing/being in its intra-activity, as Barad theorizes (2007: 235), understanding agencies of phenomena requires a cutting together/apart, or agential cut, which momentarily stabilizes the configured parts we are holding together in order to represent any given phenomenon (Barad, 2003: 46). Turning human exceptionalism on its head, Barad argues that "[i]f we thought the serious challenge, the really hard work, was taking account of *constitutive exclusions*, perhaps this awakening to the infinity of *constitutive inclusions*, the in/determinacy that manifests as virtuality calls us to a new sensibility" (2012: 13). Indeed, these constitutive inclusions begin with who and what gets to count as 'we'.

With its emphasis on moving beyond the philosophical and theoretical canon that birthed, structured, and flexed its muscles in organizing Western civilization and its abject colonies into myriad racialized, gendered, sexualized, and other stratifications, critical posthumanisms often overlap with Indigenous knowledges that precede many of posthumanism's core principles by thousands of years. Attempts at integration are messy – Indigenous scholars and knowledge holders note that much social theory, including critical posthumanism, has largely either outright ignored or digested and then re-written, Indigenous knowledges (Sundberg, 2014). For instance, Vanessa Watts contrasts posthumanism to Place-Thought, a fundamental tenet of Haudenosaunee and Anishnaabe cosmologies, which is "based upon the premise that land is alive and thinking and that humans and non-humans derive agency through the extensions of these thoughts" (2013: 21). Indigenous cosmological frameworks are embodied praxis; theories that cannot be separated from place and practice (ibid.: 22). To take another example, Deborah McGregor, Steven Whitaker, and Mahisha Sritharan note that non-humanism is embedded within Indigenous cosmologies. Water, for instance, is "understood to be a living entity with duties and obligations to ensure the well being of life, which is in direct contrast to water as a resource/property and commodity" (2020: 36). As such, water justice is not limited to human access to clean water, but water's own right to be contaminant-free. This, Julie Cruikshank (2012) points out, is not a question of culture but rather one of ontology.

## Assimilating TEK

Climate change, biodiversity loss, and other Anthropocene dividends have long concerned Indigenous communities throughout the world, who are disproportionately on the front-lines of both witnessing and experiencing these consequences. Indeed, Kyle Whyte describes climate change as "intensified colonialism":

Colonially-induced environmental changes altered the ecological conditions that supported Indigenous peoples' cultures, health, economies, and political self-determination. While Indigenous peoples, as any society, have long histories of adapting to change, colonialism caused changes at such a rapid pace that many Indigenous peoples became vulnerable to harms, from health problems related to new diets to erosion of their cultures to the destruction of Indigenous diplomacy, to which they were not as susceptible prior to colonization. Indigenous peoples often understand their vulnerability to climate change as an intensification of colonially-induced environmental changes.

(2017: 154)

Now that colonizing nations, whose development derives from the labour of peoples they violently colonized (the United States, Canada, Sweden, Denmark, the United Kingdom, France, Belgium, Germany, Spain, Russia,[2] and so on) are also experiencing some Anthropocenic effects, Western research in this area is rapidly increasing. And, indeed, there is certainly a move within environmental science to incorporate Traditional Ecological Knowledge (TEK) (Wong et al., 2020). A burgeoning number of studies emphasize the importance of using TEK to inform scientific studies of climate change as well as the populations and health of various flora and fauna.

Incorporating TEK into scientific studies aims to produce knowledge derived from the 'best of both' Western and Indigenous knowledges. The promise, here, is that these two separate systems, based on radically different cosmologies, may be meaningfully integrated and synthesized. This is a complex ambition. On the one hand, these projects may provide valuable (if mostly temporary) employment to a few Indigenous people whose local knowledge of, for instance, caribou migration patterns, is valuable to scientists. Indigenous knowledge may also indicate less invasive ways of studying animal populations, such as deriving polar bear DNA from scat rather than blood, the latter requiring invasive measures such as shooting bears with tranquillizers from helicopters (see Henri, 2012 for an extended analysis).

Notwithstanding temporary employment for a few individuals, incorporating, blending, or otherwise using TEK within an overwhelmingly Western and ongoing colonial structure may well serve the perpetuation of colonization's obsessive extraction (in this case knowledge extraction) (Sundberg, 2014; Yusoff, 2018). Moreover, incorporating TEK is, by design, partial: there are as many different Indigenous Knowledges as there are different Indigenous peoples (Smith, 2021). Isolating TEK from land, language, ways of knowing, and geography – and colonization – limits an understanding of Indigenous intellectual contributions (Martin et al., 2010; Simpson, 2004). The tendency is to generalize; to learn something about a whole lot of places rather than a whole lot about one place. By contrast, as George Manuel and Michael Posluns (1974) and Vine Deloria Jr. (1973) note, Indigenous knowledges are land-based, and as such, cannot be generalized. Moreover, applying Indigenous knowledge to ecological understanding requires researchers to dedicate themselves to questioning colonial understandings of all relationships: living and being with the land and the peoples in a life-long and evolving process of learning, which extends far beyond research granting agency time frames. This is the challenge that Tyler McCreary and Richard Milligan address, for instance, in their analysis of the ways in which industry and government recognize Indigenous ontology in negotiations over the diluted-bitumen pipeline corridor in Northern British Columbia. The authors demonstrate that this recognition,

> normalize[s] an ontology in which Indigenous difference becomes, above all, a different way of knowing, not a way of being on the land that makes that land something different, that renders that land subject to other modes of not just use but also governance.
>
> (2014: 121)

In other words, Indigenous ontology is *only* recognized in ways that are amenable to settler colonial governance and industry use.[3]

## That which is incommensurable

Many of the often cited scholars in philosophy – such as Michel Foucault, Nikolas Rose, Bruno Latour, Francisco Varela, Huberto Maturana, Timothy Morton, Gille Deleuze, and Felix Guattari, whose works are frequently taken up within posthuman analyses – typically ignore the wealth of Indigenous (and other) knowledge that preceded their meditations, despite its relevance to concepts, theories, ontologies, and epistemologies. Such is the case, for instance, with Bruno Latour's recent work on Gaia (2017). Zoe Todd (2016) attended one of Latour's talks in which much of what he said can be found in Indigenous teachings that predate his ruminations by thousands of years. As Todd observed firsthand, persistent colonial power structures are upheld through citation practices, where mainly White male philosophers and theorists are far more frequently cited than Indigenous knowledge holders, who are far less frequently cited, if at all. For Todd, though, the problem is more complex than silencing Indigenous knowledges and scholars through non-citation. This problem may be effectively addressed through revised acknowledgement and citation practices. A more insidious problem is misrepresentation; of speaking *for* Indigenous scholars

> Should I welcome his [Latour's] silence: better that he not address Indigenous thinking than to misinterpret it or distort it? As Anishinaabe and Haudenosaunee scholar Vanessa Watts (2013) points out, the appropriation

of Indigenous thinking in European contexts without Indigenous interlocutors present to hold the use of Indigenous stories and laws to account flattens, distorts and erases the embodied, legal-governance and spiritual aspects of Indigenous thinking. So there is a very real risk to Indigenous thinking being used by non-Indigenous scholars who apply it to Actor Network Theory, cosmopolitics, ontological and posthumanist threads without contending with the embodied expressions of stories, laws, and songs as bound with Indigenous-Place Thought (Watts, 2013: 31) or Indigenous self-determination.

(2016: 9)

This is a particularly damaging variation of erasure, of sustaining the abject. As Vanessa Watts argues, in order for ongoing colonialism to operationalize itself, it must attempt to make Indigenous peoples stand in disbelief of themselves and their histories. This happens, as Todd observed first-hand, each time non-Indigenous experts examine the themes we have outlined (above) that are common to posthuman approaches such as earth-human relations, human-non-human relations, relationality itself, and so on, without meaningfully engaging with Indigenous expertise. Non-engagement and engagement are, then, problematic in at least equal measure. As Todd reminds us:

So it is so important to think, deeply, about how the Ontological Turn— with its breathless 'realisations' that animals, the climate, water, 'atmospheres' and non-human presences like ancestors and spirits are sentient and possess agency, that 'nature' and 'culture', 'human' and 'animal' may not be so separate after all—is itself perpetuating the exploitation of Indigenous peoples.

(2015: 16)

One potential avenue is to acknowledge the wealth of Indigenous knowledges that precede (and are not in and of the past but active today) Western philosophy (and certainly posthumanism) and to engage with this knowledge to reverse the colonizing gaze, rather than to 'add-and-stir'. As Jeannette Armstrong considers, "[i]magine interpreting for us your own people's thinking toward us, instead of interpreting for us, our thinking, our lives, our stories" (in Regan, 2010: 235). For example, Emilie Cameron (2015) interrogates *copper stories,* or settler narratives about copper mining in the Arctic, to analyse how settler knowledges about land are constructed. And while the politics of reconciliation frames the integration of Indigenous, Black, and other subaltern knowledges with Western knowledges as eminently feasible – thus legitimizing even more (largely White colonial) scholarship to this end – decolonizing means prioritizing the dismantling of settler belief systems, rather than rendering knowledges compatible.

In their persuasive analysis of decolonizing scholarship, Eve Tuck and K. Wayne Yang (2012) argue for an "ethic of incommensurability" that recognizes a fundamental reality:

> because settler colonialism is built upon an entangled triad structure of settler-native-slave, the decolonial desires of white, nonwhite, immigrant, postcolonial, and oppressed people, can similarly be entangled in resettlement, reoccupation, and reinhabitation that actually furthers settler colonialism.
>
> (ibid.: 1)

As such, the authors argue, decolonizing strategies must, rather, "attend… to what is irreconcilable within settler colonial relations and what is incommensurable between decolonizing projects and other social justice projects" (ibid.: 4).

To put it bluntly, we have a (settler) colonial problem, not an Indigenous problem.

Just as colonial forces have (and continue to) extract and remove Indigenous objects (including flora, fauna, people and other 'goods' such as tobacco, clothing, dream catchers and so on) and settler colonial forces sanction this theft while also simultaneously occupying Indigenous territory (including universities occupying unceded Indigenous territories), so too does scholarship – including posthumanism – fetishize and otherwise 'incorporate' Indigenous knowledge (Hunt, 2014). In other words, attempting to reconcile Indigenous knowledges with Western (settler) colonial knowledge is a form of colonial erasure, or as Philip Deloria calls it, "playing Indian" (1998: 8).

As such, before we leap towards the reassurance and comfort of reconciliation, we argue that decolonizing posthumanism must pause, perhaps indefinitely, at incommensurability. *Re*conciliation is predicated on an agreement that there was, at least, at one point in time and place, consilience between Indigenous peoples and settler colonizing British and French invaders. And certainly, the Canadian government, granting agencies, and academic institutions (amongst others) are enthusiastically pushing for reconciliation in the familiar ways that colonial institutions typically do. So, for instance, in the wake of the discovery of 215 unmarked graves at a residential school in British Columbia, Prime Minister Justin Trudeau and provincial premiers, the Catholic Church, and other institutions that have systematically and relentlessly oppressed Indigenous peoples are, formulaically, calling for reconciliation between these institutions and Indigenous communities. For their part, Indigenous communities are calling for *action*: direct financial support to determine where other Indigenous children's bodies have been hidden; funding for safe and affordable housing; a health care system in Inuit Nunangat commensurate with the health care that people in southern parts of Canada enjoy; food security; hunting rights: in short, that the Crown take action on the Truth and Reconciliation Report's 94 Calls to Action. Announcing her recent decision to step down as Nunavut's only Member of Parliament, Mumilaaq Qaqqaq spoke about reconciliation from the perspective of oppressed peoples

> I think that Nunavut and Inuit in general just need to speak more truth to power. I think we need to stop allowing the federal government to give the bare minimum. Don't be thankful for getting less than what is needed. There's nothing that I am personally seeing, in my experience, that signals that the federal institution, or the RCMP institution for that matter, want to create a better relationship with Inuit and with Indigenous people ... It's a system that works because it works for itself. It doesn't work for society as a whole.... We have talked a lot about ... the housing situation, the lack of affordability and the lack of access to clean water, but we haven't talked about the why or the how, and there is such an immense amount of really pack-a-punch history in there.
>
> (CBC, 2021: np)

Commenting on the entanglement of decoloniality and posthumanism, Michalinos Zembylas argues that the way to enrich the translation of abstract ideas into policies, curricula, pedagogies, and scholarship is for academics and policy-makers to "learn how to make better use of the relative privilege that we have to become a better ally to those directly exposed to the everyday realities of coloniality — both within and beyond the academe" (2018: 264). Some, like George Sefa Dei, argue that being an ally requires active subversion of the systems within which settler colonial researchers work and live:

> I begin the discussion with what may arguably be read as a contentious statement, and maintain that within Euro-American institutions of learning conventional/traditional paradigms, differential social locations and the relative positioning of intellectual subjects constrain many of us from being subversive, resistant and challenging of dominant and/or 'stable' knowledge. Thus, to speak about Indigenous knowledges and the decolonization of the Western/Euro-American academy is to take personal and collective risks.
>
> (2002: 3)

It remains to be seen whether settler colonial institutions and structures and the people employed by them can create some form of effective 'ally' positioning that actually benefits Indigenous peoples, *according to Indigenous peoples themselves*. This is an open question rather than a foregone conclusion. Within the Canadian context, at least, Jarret Martineau and Eric Ritskes distill one of the major challenges with ally positioning:

> As anticolonial activist-intellectuals like Amilcar Cabral have warned, if all we seek is decolonization of the mind, then we will have already conceded the loss of the most precious and transformative foundation of decolonization: land and place. Theory removed from the land, removed from practice, and detached from the contexts that give it form and content propose a decolonizing strategy that risks metaphorizing its constitutive ground.
>
> (2014: ii)

Posthumanism and other fields have much to learn from Indigenous knowledge but this learning comes with a strong cautionary note. If settler colonial scholars take seriously the ontological provocations of Indigenous knowledges as more than just 'cultural', then there are myriad points of incommensurability. To take decolonizing posthumanism seriously is to refuse the comfort of reconciliation as a balm to White fragility. It is to leave awkwardly open the real possibility of the irreconcilability of knowledges, and thus the impossibility of a decolonized posthumanism within structures, systems, and processes of ongoing (settler) colonialism.

## Meanwhile, Murray Watts stakes a claim

Colonizers name Baffin Island after the first White European man to reach the coast in 1616 (Baffinland, 1963: 10). After William Baffin, subsequent self-professed explorers, such as Middleton, Ross, Parry, Boas, and Bernier, venture to the island, seeking wealth, notoriety, and a Northwest Passage to Asia but rarely venture far inland (ibid.: 10). In the early 1960s, Robert Blackader conducts aerial surveys of the interior for the Geological Survey of Canada, surveying within kilometers of *nuluujaat* (ibid.: 10). In July 1962, Murray Watts, a mining engineer, notices the outcrop during an aerial survey and determines that *nuluujaat* is made of hematite and magnetite, bearing high-grade iron ore (Baffinland, 1966: 6). Watts immediately procures prospecting permits and incorporates Baffinland Iron Mines Limited in 1963 (ibid.: 7).

## Notes

1 While there is no law on the books in Canada called "the Doctrine of Discovery", these sovereignty claims were the tacit reasoning behind Canada's ownership of land. The ownership structure formally entered Canadian law in 1888 following the St. Catherine's Milling decision (McIvor, 2021: 15), which decided that Aboriginal title over land could be revoked by the Crown at any time. The case determined

Canada's Aboriginal title policy until the *Calder decision* (discussed in Chapter 3) in 1973 (DIALOG, nd).

2 While the Russian Federation continues to engage in colonial expansion, extending the violent legacy of the USSR and the Russian Empire, the mindset underpinning expansion differs from European colonialism. To understand post-socialist patterns of Russian expansion, see Madina Tlostanova's (2015) discussion of the distinction between colonialism and imperialism.

3 Two-Eyed Seeing, for instance, is often proffered as both a viable and meaningful way forward. Albert and Murdena Marshall offer Two-Eyed Seeing as a guiding principle: "To see from one eye with the strengths of Indigenous ways of knowing, and to see from the other eye with the strengths of Western ways of knowing, and to use both of these eyes together" (2012: 335). These are parallel ways of seeing; not necessarily integrated and therefore not blended or otherwise compromised. Central to Two-Eyed Seeing is the spiritual dimension of Indigenous thought, that knowledge, as Andrea Reid and her colleagues observe "transforms the holder and that the holder bears a responsibility to act on that knowledge" (Reid et al., 2021: 249). When Two-Eyed Seeing has been taken up within Western research projects, however, words such as "weaving", "blending", "intertwining", and "integrating" are frequently used, which suggests that Two-Eyed Seeing may be serving a similar function to TEK for Western knowledge systems and research.

# 2    Reconciling geology

## Introduction

The scientist and philosopher Alfred Korzybski famously remarked that "a map is not the territory" (1958 [1931]: 750), highlighting the gap between representation and material. Nevertheless, maps were a crucial tool used to transform *terra nullius* into the territory of the British Empire. Reflecting on the mapping of the Arctic archipelago, geologist A. P. Low wrote, "[t]he great land masses of the Arctic islands have now been outlined, and all that remains to be done is to fill in minor details" (1906: 72). Those "the minor details" Low and his team set out to complete were instrumental in establishing resource extraction as the central tension in Crown/Inuit relations. In effect, the map *does* make the colonial territory.

This chapter examines the history of the Geological Survey of Canada's (GSC) exploration of the Eastern Arctic, focusing on the 1903–1904 Arctic survey conducted by A. P. Low. The GSC was founded to map this tenuously held land, with the explicit intention of identifying sites for Canadian mining. Expanding on Kathryn Yusoff's argument that "there is not geology on one hand and stories about geology on the other" (2018: 34), this chapter explores the role geological surveys played in settler colonial expansion and how geology in Canada was (and continues to be) used to create and uphold racialised colonial relations of power and dispossession. This case study depicts pre-reconciliation mineral relations rooted in free entry, self-conscious displays of sovereignty, and the racist categorization and study of Inuit. As well as planting flags throughout the Arctic Archipelago to establish Canadian possession and sovereignty materially and symbolically, the geological mapping survey also studied and mapped Inuit – their bodies, behaviours, nomadic patterns, and family relations to establish a colonial subject position in relation to the settler geo-logics of the occupying state. We analyse the survey team's notes on Inuit – notes presented as part of geologic observations – through Yusoff's theory of inhumanism, arguing that the survey conflated Inuit with geology and inhuman matter by observing and writing about their lives and culture in the same fashion as the rocks. This matters: the GSC was integral to cementing Canada's legal claim to rights of "discovery", through the application of

DOI: 10.4324/9781003342526-3

geology, and set the stage for mineral negotiations within the Nunavut Land Claims Agreement.

## Geological stories

Commenting on the Anthropocene's proclamations of "sudden concern with the exposures of environmental harm to white liberal communities" (2018: 10), Kathryn Yusoff argues that these harms have always been intentionally exported to Black and Indigenous communities "under the rubric of civilization, progress, modernization, and capitalism" (ibid). Throughout *A Billion Black Anthropocenes or None*, Yusoff critiques the role of geology in the formation of subaltern subject positions:

> While the search for geologic resources instigated the imperative to enslave, geology quickly established itself as an imperial science that both organized the extraction of the Americas and, in the continued context of Victorian colonialism, became a structuring priority in the colonial complex, especially in India, Canada, and Australia. These territories became organized as material resources and markets for Empire, and the geologic practices established in these colonies continued to underwrite current neocolonial extraction processes by Canada and Australia throughout the world (Canada, for example, is the largest national global mining corporation). The ownership of strata and the surface–subsurface bifurcation in Australia and Canada by the Crown continue to unsettle native title and reservation lands. Thus the classificatory logics of geology have implications for ongoing colonialism.
>
> (2018: 89)

Inhumanism acknowledges and centres the history of colonialism and the racial power dynamics while introducing the role of geology, a historically understudied aspect of discourses of power. Central to Yusoff's theory is geology as a relation of power and fundamentally constitutive in racialized relations of power, supported by histories of slavery and settler-colonial genocide: geology is inseparable from the subjugation of Black and Indigenous peoples. Yusoff argues that the practice of geology, and the establishment of the discipline, is literally (i.e. not metaphorically) foundational to the colonial state and the project of extraction and racialization. She states, "…there is an axis of power and performance that meets within these geologic objects and the narratives they tell about the human story" (ibid: 34). In other words, the structures of power created and enacted to enable extraction through dispossession, and the enslavement of Black and Indigenous peoples, are inextricable from our creation of the geologic and subsequently, the technologies built on the use of minerals, from coal-powered steam engines to lithium-ion batteries: these objects contain the politics of their extraction. Fundamentally,

Yusoff's theory of inhumanism hinges on exposing the practice of geology as organized to expose Black and Indigenous communities to harm. Her argument makes clear that both Black peoples and Indigenous peoples have been "caught and defined in the ontological wake of geology" (ibid: 14).

Yusoff further critically argues that Indigenous peoples have been rendered inhuman matter through the ontological flattening of geology (ibid; also see Yusoff, 2013, 2017, 2021; Clark and Yusoff, 2017). That is, geology's categorization of Indigenous peoples *along with* minerals rendered equivalent (non-White) human and inhuman. In this chapter, we extend Yusoff's chronicles of the history of British geologic surveying as essential to the establishment of settler colonialism to the GSC. Our case study considers how the classificatory logics of geology ordered Crown/Inuit relations and structured ongoing colonialism.

## Enabling extraction

Since its founding in 1841, the Geological Survey of Canada has been a purposeful and key tool in enabling and incentivizing the resource extraction industry, providing information to the industry about the likely occurrence of minerals to triangulate the efforts of private prospecting[1] (Zaslow, 1975). The anticipation of mineral wealth shaped Canada's settler-colonial government, as it promised capitalist expansion beyond an agrarian economy. Through the GSC, the Crown operationalized the search for mineral wealth. Morris Zaslow summarizes the integral relationship: "Beyond question, the Survey has been a significant force in the Canadian mining industry's rise to its present prominence, and it has assisted the economic growth of the nation in a major way" (ibid: 4). Or, as geographer Jason William Grek Martin puts it more directly, "[t]he work of the GSC transformed remote land into legible territory ready to exploit by settlers, miners, traders, and other extractive industries" (2009: ii). Take Treaty 8, which covers Northern Alberta, parts of British Columbia, Saskatchewan, the Northwest Territories, and the Yukon, for example. The Treaty negotiation process began in 1870, after the GSC mapped petroleum resources – known as the tar sands today (Preston, 2013: 47). Signed in 1899, the Treaty secured access to economically valuable resources for the Crown while limiting the rights of Cree and Dene (ibid: 47). In effect, the survey provided intelligence on where to operationalize Indigenous dispossession.

While the GSC was founded in 1841, it would take decades before the Arctic archipelago was traversed by its classifying logic – the Arctic was ignored and unmapped by the GSC until 1904 when the Crown's sovereignty was threatened. Canada's claim to the Arctic Archipelago region derived from two territorial transfers from Britain, first in 1870 which covered the former territories of the Hudson's Bay Company (known as Rupert's Land) and the Northwestern Territory, and another in 1880 that included all other British territorial rights in the Arctic (Scace, 1975: 8). Britain's claim derived from

Martin Frobisher's 1577 "discovery" of Baffin Island (see Chapter 1), supported by the presence of British citizens starting with the establishment of Fort Charles in 1668 (ibid: 8), and the ongoing presence of British whalers (ibid: 8). Other foreign nations had planted other flags throughout the Arctic and contested Britain's claim (ibid) – thus Britain transferred "ownership" of tenuously held lands to Canada. Further, the boundaries of the transferred regions were ill-defined, described in the Governor General's 1895 order-in-council as having an "indefinite extent" (in ibid: 14) – and while Britain's 1895 Colonial Boundaries Act provided the rough legal framework for Canadian sovereignty in the Arctic (Ross, 1976: 88), mapping the territory and making a show of occupation would cement the claim.

Canada's claim was repeatedly brought into question in the following years through disputes around the 1897–1898 Yukon gold rush, Norwegian explorer Otto Sverdrup's 1902 claim to several Arctic islands, and losing a 1904 boundary dispute with the United States over Alaska (Scace, 1975: 14). These disputes became a media scandal and the geologists of the GSC joined the fray, arguing that an Arctic survey would assert sovereignty in the region (Ross, 1976: 89). The 1903–1904 GSC expedition, led by A. P. Low, was a corrective to questions of ownership, serving to map the territory while simultaneously declaring sovereignty (Blackadar, 1976: 11). In effect, the government-funded survey aimed to signal that the state's power to map the territory extended to the power to govern the territory (Grek-Martin, 2009: ii). Further, the survey intersected with, and forever changed the lives of, Inuit. Beyond asserting land sovereignty, the GSC teams asserted sovereignty over Indigenous people:

> Operating usually in districts still dominated by Indians and Eskimos [sic], fur traders and missionaries, the reconnaissance geologists prepared reports that directed the future lumberman [sic], miner, and farmer who came to develop the natural wealth and extend the blessings (or defects) of western civilization, technology, and society to an undeveloped land. Almost everywhere they went in the north, *field officers found themselves in the position of being the very first advance agents of Dominion government authority.* In 1887 they led the way to the occupation by Canada of its distant Yukon frontier. From the reconnaissance explorers like Dawson and Bell came frequent warnings to the government of the need to assert Canadian sovereignty and authority in the interests of the nation in general, *and the native inhabitants in particular.* Now, in 1903–04, they were again in the lead, proclaiming the Dominion's authority over the last frontier, the islands of Canada's Arctic.
>
> (Zaslow, 1975: 175, emphasis added)

As such, geology and the larger story about geology – the discovery of land, the building of a nation, and the dispossession of Indigenous peoples – are one and the same. Low's published account of his journey, *The Cruise of the*

*Neptune, the Dominion Government Expedition to Hudson Bay and the Arctic Islands on Board the D.G.S. Neptune, 1903 – 1904* (1906), demonstrates how minerals, land, and Indigenous inhabitants were all conflated in the pursuit of sovereignty. The survey team set sail from Halifax on August 23, 1903, on the steamship Neptune. In addition to scientific research, the survey aided "in the establishment, on the adjoining shores, of permanent stations for the collection of customs, the administration of justice and the enforcement of the law as in other parts of the Dominion" (ibid: 12). Major J. D. Moodie, of the Northwest Mounted Police, travelled with Low's team as the newly appointed Acting Commissioner of the unorganized Northwestern Territories, the lands for which the Crown had not yet established functional local governance. The team claimed Canadian sovereignty by regulating foreign whalers, planting flags in remote islands, and espousing the effects of Canadian law to Inuit families (Ross, 1976). As they sailed throughout the island, the team would periodically stop to read aloud "a document taking formal possession in the name of King Edward VII., for the Dominion", then raise a flag, salute the flag, and bury the document in a stone cairn (Low, 1906: 48).

Low's account, of course, also covers the geology of the islands. Chapter VIII covers the geological history of the region – the succession of rocks, periods of glaciation, and so on – while Chapter IX covers the specific mineral occurrences by region with a section on economic minerals. GSC publications include speculations on the occurrence of valuable minerals to triangulate prospecting efforts. Low details the areas where gold, silver, copper, iron, mica, graphite, molybdenite, lignite, and coal might be found. While Low is a scientist, working to expand the knowledge of geology in the region, it is clear that when he writes about "important mineral deposits" (ibid: 237), the importance he speaks to is in the interest of expanding Canada's industrial reach through inventorying the geology of the Arctic Archipelago – Low's team extended the power of the state to the Arctic's land and people; *both* for industrial development. In a time of public doubt about the Government's ability to hold onto the Arctic, "the work of a publicly-funded scientific survey was a profound symbol of authority because a state's power to explore and map its national territory signified its power to rule over that territory" (Grek-Martin, 2009: ii). The maps and reports produced by the GSC, and by Low's survey, discursively framed the Arctic Archipelago as Canada's territory and enabled ongoing dispossession of Inuit land. As such, geology is a subtle tool of statecraft, that "has a lower resolution or a more subterranean subjective operation than more performative biopolitics, but it nonetheless continues to be oppressive in its extraction qualities" (Yusoff, 2018: 81). The guise of a scientific survey lends neutral credibility to Low's survey but when the Inuit organization ITC commissioned a chapter on "The History of Foreign Activities" (read: European invasion) within a 1975 report on Arctic resource use, it remembers Low not as a scientist but as an agent of the federal government, staking a claim to the land (Scace, 1975: 16).

## Mapping the Inuit body

As Yusoff argues, "geology is a mode of accumulation, on one hand, and of dispossession, on the other, depending on which side of the geologic color line you end up on" (2018: 14). In Canada, Indigenous peoples most definitively ended up on the dispossession line. The resource extraction industry depends on surveys to aid in the accumulation of mineral wealth while dispossessing Inuit and other Indigenous peoples through the racialized geology of Empire – Low's field report is a case study of dispossession operationalized. Through geology, land, ecologies, and racialized people, "became subject to encoding as inhuman property, as a tactic of empire and European world building" (ibid: 75). The GSC and other colonial institutions worked in concert to systematically transform the vast Arctic Archipelago into property to extract minerals to create wealth for European settlers in the nascent colonial nation. In what follows, we analyse how Low and his team related to Inuit. The practices of the GSC team served to align Inuit with the inhuman through these interrelated but also distinct modes of categorization, contributing to an ongoing policy position from the Canadian government that regarded Inuit *themselves as natural resources* (Duffy, 1988).

Chapter IV of Low's report, *A Historical Summary of the Discoveries and Explorations in Arctic America*, summarized the history of the Arctic expeditions of White men, beginning with Frobisher in 1576. In his writing, European scientists are named individuals and Inuit are grouped together, unnamed and *en masse*. The chapters on Inuit (called by the racist slur Eskimo in the Report) are structured similarly to chapters on geological inventories themselves. Indeed, Low devoted a nearly equivalent portion of his report to detailing Inuit lives (52 pages) as he did geological observations (65 pages), cataloguing belief systems and measuring and photographing Inuit. This parallels the writing of Sir Charles Lyell, President of the Geological Survey of London, who similarly intertwined geological writing with racial propositions. Yusoff notes Lyell's writing moves between "'Geology and Cretaceous strata' and 'Montgomery. Curfew. Sunday School for Negros' in one chapter … and 'Distinct Table [sic] for Coloured and White Passengers' and 'Fossil Shells' in another" (in Yusoff, 2018: 81). These geologists drew no distinction "between social and geologic strata with regard to the language of property" (ibid: 82) when the colour line established by the geologist's colonialism had been drawn. The appendix of Low's account includes charts detailing the size of Inuit bodies prepared by his travelling companion Dr. Borden, along with extensive photographs documenting clothing, homes, and tools. The team continuously studied Inuit physiology, in the same manner as the rocks, flora, and fauna:

> Geological examinations were made on these land journeys, as well as at every ship's halt, and large collections were made of rocks and fossils,

northern birds, eggs and nests, skins and skeletons of animals, fishes and marine invertebrates, and plants and insects. *Eskimos* [sic] *were studied, and a census was taken.* Observations were recorded of the weather, ice conditions and movements, tides and currents, and the habitats and distribution of the whales, seals, walrus, caribou, and muskox of the region.

(Zaslow, 1975: 173, emphasis added)

Low and his compatriots saw no difference in observing the tides and measuring the people, aligning Inuit with the landscape. Moreover, the sovereignty Low's team asserted over the territory, gained by planting flags, was extended to sovereignty over Inuit through policing. To wit, Major Moodie, a member of the Northwest Mounted Police (NWMP), travelled north with the scientists to establish a permanent police presence. The Crown granted broad administrative powers to the NWMP, in the stated interest of disrupting foreign whalers (Ross, 1976), but in Inuit affairs, they were effectively an occupying police force that forever reshaped communities (Qikiqtani Inuit Association, 2013). Major Moody arranged a ceremony for local Inuit families and offered gifts along with an explanation of the structure of the Dominion of Canada and the British Empire:

> The Major had about eight gallons of tea made and with five pounds of hard tack and other biscuits soon disappeared. A clay pipe and a bit of tobacco was given to each of the twenty-five natives [sic] present. Then through the interpreter the Major told the natives that there was a big chief over them all who had many tribes of different colours and how this big chief, who was King Edward VII, had the welfare of all his peoples at heart. King Edward wanted them all to do what was right and good, and had sent the Major as his personal representative or in other words the King could not come himself so 'I was to act for him'! The Major wanted them to do what was right and good and to settle all quarrels but he would punish all offenders.

(Borden, 1903–1904: 38)

Like the flag-raising on the islands, the survey team brought police to claim ownership of all Inuit through a brief display; a short spectacle preceding the imposition of colonial law. As such, policing and the monarchy were (partially) described to a few Inuit individuals before being forcibly imposed on the entire population. The Canadian effort to claim the geologic resources of the Arctic and the bodily resources of Inuit, who were nevertheless expected to hunt and guide survey teams, and eventually provide manual labour in mines and military outposts, share a natal moment. Maps, declared as neutral artifacts of science, obscure colonial geologic relations: "those lines on a map and the collections of mineral artifacts they enable have consequences; they establish unfolding geo-logics, for particular bodies and subject positions, as disposable in the shadow economy of extraction" (Yusoff, 2018: 66). Inuit were cast as another piece of the ceded territory, claimed by Frobisher more than 400 years previous, fungible within extractive capitalism.

In an extraordinarily violent addition to an already violent colonization, the survey aligned Inuit with the inhuman through the extraction and theft of human remains. Dr. Borden, a medical doctor with the survey team, detailed his ongoing collection of Inuit skeletons in his diary. His collection began with "a very well preserved skull – no doubt, of a very ancient Eskimo [sic]" (Borden, 1903–1904: 102). Borden lamented that another team member found a skull but did not bring it back to the boat (ibid: 103). While some skulls he found did not end up in his collection as they were allegedly too fresh (ibid: 117), Borden wrote about taking the entire body of an Inuk woman – he wrote: "it was a pretty hard, nasty job but it will make a fine skeleton & is now sunk in the sea to be cleaned" (ibid: 106). During the survey, human bone collection happened alongside rock collection. This practice isn't unique to Borden – "for centuries Western scientists have disinterred Aboriginal human remains and cultural items for collection and study" (Blair, 2005: 1). Human remains removed from Indigenous burial grounds have little protection under Canadian law (ibid: 10). The extraction of bodies imposed the same classificatory logic of geology to people – what is in the ground can be claimed by the right of discovery, by being the first, by being superior, by drawing a sharp line between who is human and who is not – it is the racialization of matter that equates Indigenous life (and the death of ancestors) with the inhuman (Yusoff, 2018). Borden's extraction of bodies for classification in his laboratory exemplifies how colonial science served to establish racial categories in Canada. From the metaphorical categorization within Low's text to Moody's symbolic move towards sovereignty, to Borden's literal extraction of Inuit bones; each aligned Inuit with the inhuman and served as justification for ongoing and expanded extraction by the settler-colonial state.

While the stated purpose – and the historical legacy – of the Neptune survey was an inventory of minerals, it functioned on multiple levels as a tool of colonial dispossession, by using the organization and categorization of minerals to enact racialization (Yusoff, 2018) on Inuit populations. The geological relations first established by Martin Frobisher, and expanded by Low and the GSC, underpinned eventual Inuit land claim negotiations, ensuring that territory and mineral resources were the central negotiation pieces.

## Conclusions

It all seems a bit ridiculous when we imagine it: a group of foreign White men standing alone on the shore of an island, trying to find somewhere to stake their flag amidst the rocks. The performative nature of these forays is captured in geologist Robert Blackadar's recounting of his 1953 encounter with Robert Peary's flag:

> The day we spotted the cairn, Hattersley-Smith proposed we follow a tra-
> dition of British fair play: we would walk towards our find hand-in-hand
> so neither of us could later say, "I was first to discover Peary's flag!" Hid-
> den in the cairn was a rusted tin with a perfectly preserved remnant of
> the flag the size of a handkerchief. Later we gave it to Peary's widow.
> Hattersley-Smith and I made other finds that year. We found tins of fruit-
> cake from an 1875 British expedition, and letters addressed to Amundsen
> left behind by a Danish team in 1920. And we began the work of mapping
> the Canadian Arctic. It was a mammoth task that took years to complete,
> over hundreds of thousands of square miles. In the end, we planted our
> own Canadian flag, and established that we – no less than Americans or
> Russians – had a stake in the Arctic.
>
> (Blackadar, nd: np)

But these actions, however theatrical, have legal standing. The Crown's pursuit of sovereignty was about building a legal case that Britain, and subsequently Canada, had the right to claim Indigenous lands. As such, the GSC
Neptune mission was not a neutral scientific act of filling in "the minor details" but rather a deliberate and planned act of dispossession that aligned
Inuit with inhuman geological matter. In its pursuit of serving the mining
industry, the GSC used geology as a tool of empire to assert an elusive *sovereignty* throughout the Arctic archipelago. S*overeignty* in Canada is always
a euphemism for the Doctrine of Discovery (McIvor, 2021: 18). Low's flags
mirror the flags that came before, serving as the legal justification for an-
nexing land – this justification informs everything about Crown/Indigenous
relations (ibid: 16).

## Meanwhile, Baffinland gathers support to develop the Mary River Mine

Senior members of the federal government invest heavily in Arctic resource
extraction, including Baffinland's iron claims. Exploratory drilling begins
in 1963, aided in large part by subsidies totalling nearly $25 million from
the Department of Energy, Mines and Resources (Duffy, 1988: 176). Baffinland reports the mountain contains an estimated 120 million tons of iron ore,
averaging 68.13% purity (Baffinland, 1966: 7) – among the richest deposits
ever staked (Baffinland, nd). The company seeks funding to develop the site
into a new mine, named for the adjoining Mary River – the financial models
show it is not economically viable in the present market (ibid: 1). The federal
government, predicting future profit, continues to support the operation. At

the opening of the 51st Session of the NWT Council in 1970, minister of Indian Affairs and Northern Development (who later becomes Canada's Prime Minister), Jean Chretien, proclaims, "The potential of the north is surely limitless ... I think of the mountains of rich ore at Mary River ... uneconomic today but not tomorrow" (in Duffy, 1988: 177).

Around this time, Minister Chretien is also making waves with his White Paper, a policy paper dedicated to assimilating Indigenous peoples into settler society, sparking backlash from First Nations, Metis, and Inuit across Canada. Inuit organize national gatherings, starting with the 1970 Coppermine Conference of Inuit to discuss potential responses to profoundly increasing pressures to assimilate/disappear (McPherson, 2003: 51). For the first time, a land claim process is seriously considered, and in 1971 Inuit Tapirisat of Canada (ITC) is founded as a national voice for Inuit, setting the negotiations in motion (ibid: 63). A major first hurdle: within Inuit cosmology, people cannot own land: ownership is a colonial concept.

## Note

1 The survey exists within a broader set of policies that enable resource extraction in Canada. Through a permissive legal framework for exploration – "free entry" – prospectors have been allowed "to go anywhere, secretly if necessary, to explore Crown land" (McPherson: 38). Free entry in Canada is derived from a centuries-old staking system in British tin mining districts, which eventually formed the basis of British law and was formalized in Canada with the 1859 BC Gold Fields Act, which was the basis of the Yukon Quartz Act, and later informed the writing of mining legislation in the Northwest Territories (Hoogeveen, 2015: 125). Entry to land in Canada is "free" in that prospectors/the resource extraction industry can stake a claim without consulting anyone – including Indigenous peoples (ibid: 127).

# 3 Reconciling resource extraction

*Figure 3.1* Relationship to the Land (Use Planning Provisions), 2021 by Hillary Predko. Cotton thread, felt, and seal fur on linen. 100 cm × 100 cm.

## Another mapping exercise

When I (Hillary) began this research years ago, I struggled to understand how the 1993 Nunavut Land Claims Agreement (NCLA) created Inuit Owned Lands (IOL). The Inuit of Nunavut collectively own IOL and manage these lands via regional Inuit beneficiary organizations. Written out, the area sounds

DOI: 10.4324/9781003342526-4

unimaginably vast – 87,968,000 acres of land for surface use activities, and 9,264,000 acres of land for subsurface mining rights (McPherson, 2003: 271) – but mapped out, IOL is sparse. Indeed, most of Nunavut – about 80% of the territory – is Crown Land. The Crown also retains mineral rights to 98% of the territory (NTI, nd: 3). Nunavut Tunngavik Inc. (NTI, nd) reproduces the IOL map again and again – in mining reports and in government documents. So, I set out to reproduce the map one more time, in thread and cloth, as a research-creation (Loveless, 2019) exercise to deepen my engagement with the work. The map is a testament to the central role resource extraction holds in Nunavut, or as political scientist Ailsa Henderson establishes, "[t]he land on which Canadian Inuit live has been described as barren and inhospitable, but this mistakes temperature for resources" (2007: 19). I questioned how IOL was defined within the NCLA and unfolded the broader story of comprehensive land claims in Canada, which serve settler/colonial neoliberal capitalist goals.

On an inky indigo square of cloth, I outlined the boundaries of Nunavut in white thread, tracing the crinkled fjords of the Arctic Archipelago. I spent ten months (physically confined to my apartment by COVID-19 restrictions) embroidering the parcels of IOL, with bright sections of pink and red thread contrasting with the dark background. The little French knots of my embroidery started looking like a tundra populated with cloudberries, so I added a figure in a parka (made with gifted seal skin harvested in Panniqtuuq), picking berries. A settler-colonial view of Nunavut sees the land as a mapped territory. By contrast that is as much ideological as it is material, John Amagoalik, one of the Inuit leaders who established the Nunavut lands claim, said this:

> What is important to remember though, is that the Inuit do not consider their lands as "property" but rather as "home". But it is not a home which has been obtained by making a down payment and signing a legal document. It is not a home around which we built a fence. The Government of Canada says all this land belongs to the "Crown". It is seen by the government as "property" which can be leased, rented, auctioned and sold. The government is interested in the North because it has resources which can be exploited, not because it is home.
>
> (1978: 4)

I hope that the inclusion of a human figure changes the perspective on the map, turning the god's eye view of a territory made for resource extraction into a landscape that is a little less familiar to the colonial eye. To the Crown and resource extraction industries, the land is property; to Inuit, land is home. With this literally material project, I am trying to denaturalize the relationalities that govern our current extractivist systems of exploitation and power by making visible a set of power relations, entrenched in lines drawn on maps and lengthy agreements that afforded the dispossession of Inuit lands. In effect, this artwork is an exploration of how we might take an ethic of incommensurability (Tuck and Yang, 2012; see also Chapter 1) seriously when considering these ontological positions. The creation of this work is also an exercise in materializing situated knowledges (Haraway, 1988), an exploration in critical mapping, exploring our own relationship as Canadian settlers to Indigenous land thousands of kilometres from where we live. Exploring the contours of IOL through embroidery led us to inquire into the formation of these boundaries and question their effectiveness.

Art making opens up productive spaces for navigating the complexity of settler/Indigenous relationships and "demonstrate[s] that there is no single perspective on the Anthropocene, no collective 'we' who experience the Anthropocene in the same ways and with the same kinds of costs, an observation that holds across categories of the human and more-than-human" (Tsing et al., 2021). Natalie Loveless describes how artistic research (commonly referred to as research-creation in Canada, and practice-based research elsewhere) attends to the urgent questions of the humanities and posthumanities through "modes of sensuous, aesthetic attunement, and work as a conduit to focus attention, elicit public discourse, and shape cultural imaginaries" (2019: 16). As such, this tapestry contributes to an emerging opus that incorporates practice-based processes of knowledge production within the humanities and societies.

## The Crown: Asymmetrical exchange

In the following section, we summarize the government of Canada's comprehensive land claims strategy, and the historical context surrounding the 1993 NLCA. We argue that the creation of IOL, while an example of skillful negotiation on the part of Inuit leaders involved, exemplifies how comprehensive land claims further the Canadian government's commitment to resource extraction, and ultimately affect dispossession. From the 1920s to the 1970s, the Crown presumed that land not explicitly covered by treaties or private property was Crown Land – an assumption upended by the 1973 *Calder decision.*[1] The ruling underscored the fact that Canada had no legal grounds for its sovereignty claims to land, or "no reason in law as to why Canadian territory should be Canada's to govern" (Lowman and Barker, 2015: 3), prompting anxious policies that would reestablish the "certainty" of Crown ownership. The NLCA negotiations, therefore, followed a shift in Crown/Indigenous land relations wherein "colonial relations of power are no longer reproduced primarily through overtly coercive means, but rather through the asymmetrical exchange of mediated forms of state recognition and accommodation" (Coulthard, 2014: 15). We must keep in mind that the federal government is always prepared to use force when "asymmetrical exchange" fails to secure the desired outcome (access to land). From deploying the army to subdue Mohawk of Kanehsatà:ke and protect private property development in the 1990s, to ongoing RCMP raids on Wet'suwet'en land defenders blocking the development of the Coastal GasLink pipeline today, state violence is ready-to-hand if other forms of discipline fail (Foucault, 1977).

Comprehensive land claims are a demonstration of disciplinary power (ibid) whereby the exchange remains asymmetrical – these negotiations serve to undermine Indigenous peoples' sovereign power and access to land. As Bruce McIvor, partner at First Peoples Law LLP, explains

> According to the federal government, the objective of its new land claims policy was to reconcile Indigenous Peoples' Aboriginal title and rights with the interests of non-Indigenous Canada. From the federal government's perspective, reconciliation is about achieving "certainty" for "economic and resource development."
>
> (2021: 98)

As Chapter 2 details, Crown "interests'" is a colonial euphemism: "Every time Canadians read in the news about 'reconciliation' they are entering a national conversation based on the racist and duhumanizing Doctrine of Discovery" (ibid: 17). As such, the map of IOL resembles the GSC maps that aided prospectors in their search for minerals. The parcels of IOL, particularly subsurface parcels, are presented as an inventory of minerals to be extracted – they document land *ownership*. In recreating this map, and analysing the history of its production, we argue that the NCLA ensured increasing resource extraction IOL: in short, the comprehensive land claims process is a contemporary form of dispossession, cast as reconciliation. The consolation prize: the opportunity to develop mines on whatever lands have not been ceded to the Crown. Resource extraction, in other words, at all costs.

## The Nunavut agreement and the comprehensive lands claims process

The 1993 NLCA is the largest Indigenous land claim in Canadian history (McPherson, 2003). It defines a broad set of rights and outlines its territorial administration.[2] The role that minerals played in the negotiations is frequently acknowledged but underexplored, with the notable exception of geologist Robert McPherson's *New Owners in Their Own Land* (2003). McPherson was hired to assess mineral potential by ITC during land claims negotiations in the early 1990s and later wrote a detailed history of resource development in the territory. This section gives an overview of how the comprehensive land claims process inscribed the central role of resource extraction in Nunavut and overwrote a more holistic vision for Nunavut brought forward by Inuit leaders early in the negotiations (Amagoalik, 1978).

The development of natural resources has been the driving force behind the Arctic's expansion and annexation, with policies "designed to extract and exploit the northern resources as inexpensively and with as little interference as possible from the people who live north of the 60th parallel" (Amagoalik, 1978: 5). Inuit have a unique history with the Canadian state that has vacillated "between well-meaning if ill-judged paternalism and outright cultural assimilation" (Henderson, 2007: 23). By 1925, Inuit were considered wards of the state, when Charles Stewart, Minister of the Interior, argued before Parliament that since the federal government governed Inuit through trials, imprisonment, and execution, it must take responsibility for community well-being (Duffy, 1988: 7). Importantly, the Indian Act did not include Inuit, and parliament declared in 1930 that Inuit would have full status as Canadian citizens (ibid: 11). In practice, the government "appeared to regard [Inuit] as part of the natural resources of the region" (ibid: 11). In 1936, the Department of Mines and Resources was tasked with the "administration" of Inuit affairs (ibid: 11). From the 1950s and into the 1970s, United States government and industry exploration activity in the Arctic reached an unprecedented level, with oil and gas drilling beginning in Prudhoe Bay, Alaska. In Canada, the federal government wanted to expand resource extraction and offered subsidies to extractive industries for expansion, including exploration assistance grants (McPherson, 2003: 45). For Inuit, resisting resource exploitation became the catalyst for political organizing:

> …in the 1950s, led by the governments, [white people] began to search the land and waters for hidden wealth. Tracked giant vehicles left ruts across the land, seismic explosions shook the silent grip of nature at regular intervals, and expansive white entrepreneurs and engineers talked grandly of resource extraction projects that would overwhelm and change the North. From the beginning, then, Inuit expressed their political concerns in relation to land.
>
> (Merritt, 1989: 3)

The 1970s energy politics "fueled an aggressive push by state and industry to develop what it saw as the largely untapped resource potential (natural gas, minerals, and oil) of northern Canada" (Coulthard, 2014: 6). The 1970s also marked a new era of Indigenous land claims in Canada, and Inuit organizers saw land claims as a pathway (within the hegemonic colonial system) to limiting resource extraction's reach.

To understand comprehensive land claims policy, we must consider the Crown's position on Indigenous land ownership in the 1970s, Aboriginal title[3] in common law, and the implications of the 1973 Calder decision. Comprehensive land claims are often called modern treaties, as the Government of Canada ceased treaty negotiations in 1923 following the 'numbered treaties' negotiated in Western Canada (Bernauer, 2019: 254). Treaties entail negotiating the exchange of Aboriginal title, which is "the way in which the common law recognizes Aboriginal land rights" (Chief Justice Lamer in McNeil, 1997: 119). Aboriginal title is collective ownership of land deriving from occupation, use, and control of land, and is legally recognized as an inherent right (McNeil, 1997). Importantly, as Lamer acknowledges, Aboriginal title is a concept within British common law – it does not map onto Indigenous people's conceptions of their own lands, traditions, or values. The Crown first recognized Aboriginal title in the Royal Proclamation of 1763 (Irwin, 2018: np). As such, treaties were the means to purchase Aboriginal title rights and gain Crown sovereignty (ibid).

The Crown assumed that Aboriginal title had been disrupted across the country following the numbered treaties: the activities that constitute Aboriginal title had been thoroughly upended – even those communities that had never signed treaties had changed settlement patterns and no longer had full control over their land. The infamous 1969 White Paper, *Statement of the Government of Canada on Indian Policy*, argued that land claims between the Crown and Indigenous peoples were of no use because Indigenous peoples didn't have anything *to claim*:

> …[A]boriginal claims to land … are so general and un-defined that it is not realistic to think of them as specific claims capable of remedy except through a policy and program that will end injustice to the Indians as members of the Canadian community.
>
> (in Godlewska and Webber, 2007: 8).

The White Paper aimed to eliminate any legal distinction between Indigenous peoples and settlers, including any distinct legal relationship to land. In short, it sought to entrench the Crown's position that Aboriginal title no longer existed, Indigenous peoples had no property rights, and that treaties were unnecessary (ibid: 8).

In 1973, Canada's Supreme Court *Calder* decision eroded that position. Frank Calder, president of the Nisga'a Tribal Council and lead plaintiff in the case, campaigned for the recognition of Nisga'a Aboriginal title rights (ibid: 1). Six of the seven Supreme Court justices affirmed that continued use of land qualifies as evidence of Aboriginal title (Bernauer, 2019: 255). The Court was split three to three on the legal foundations of title and whether it still existed (Godlewska and Webber, 2007: 4). The case was ultimately a defeat for the Nisga'a – the nation "had not secured permission to sue the Crown, which at that time was still required in British Columbia" (ibid: 4) – ultimately the court did not recognize Nisga'a Aboriginal title at the time. However, the ruling did substantially increase the remit of Aboriginal title interpretation:

> Six of the seven judges had decided that Aboriginal title existed as a right within the common law, regardless of whether it had been recognized by the government or acknowledged in any treaty. Moreover, they decided that Aboriginal title existed not just in territories under European influence

at the time of the Royal Proclamation – that is, in eastern Canada and the prairies, where it had already been largely addressed through treaties.

(ibid: 5)

Upon hearing the ruling, Prime Minister Pierre Elliot Trudeau remarked, "maybe [Indigenous peoples] have more rights than we thought" (in Lukacs, 2019: 149). The Crown was compelled to come to the negotiating table and reconsider land claims. In effect, the Calder decision meant that Indigenous peoples who had never signed a treaty, like Inuit, could make a legal case for owning their land. Trudeau's government *could* (see Chapter 5 for a list of further 'coulds') have embraced Aboriginal title rights, sought to strengthen the laws protecting them, and simply affirmed ownership but opted instead to develop a strategy of elimination:

> Established under Trudeau in the aftermath of the Calder decision, the Comprehensive Land Claims policy was designed to bring the land securely back under the legal control of the Canadian government. The policy would offer First Nations and Inuit cash-for-land deals, taking advantage of their poverty and the duress they felt as resource companies moved unhindered into their territories. Since the 1970s, this policy has undergone small alterations, but its core purpose has remained the same: land rights "extinguishment", the ugliest term in the linguistic arsenal of the state.
>
> (ibid: 149)

Land claims could have been an opportunity to affirm ongoing Indigenous ownership of land. But instead, they continue to intentionally serve dispossession. In effect, comprehensive land claims, as detailed in the 1973 *Statement on Claims of Indian and Inuit people: a federal native claims policy*, offer "a limited set of rights and benefits" (Coulthard, 2014: 66) if Indigenous nations agree to "extinguish" the broad and undefined rights of Aboriginal title. This renders Crown land ownership "certain". It, of course, ignores the fact that "achieving 'certainty' through extinguishment is anathema to the very basis of Aboriginal title" (McIvor, 2021: 100). The lands that Indigenous nations do retain become private property – as with the fee-simple ownership of IOL – inscribing a neoliberal model of ownership that "ignores key differences in Indigenous, state, and private proprietary interests in land" (Pasternak, 2014: 181). Further, these agreements effectively submit authority over fee-simple lands to Canada through property law (ibid: 190). The outcome of comprehensive land claims agreements is a much more limited form of land ownership than Aboriginal title.

With myriad downsides, it's easy to lose sight of why Indigenous peoples entered (and continue to enter) land claims negotiations with the Crown: the status quo is untenable, and no better options appear on the settler colonial table. Within this settler/colonial system, Indigenous peoples are required to satisfy the vague requirements of the courts to prove Aboriginal title and begin a land claim. Establishing proof requires an often insurmountable high bar:

> Among other caveats, [A]boriginal rights to land can only be claimed if it can be proved to the satisfaction of Settler Canadian officials that the land in question is part of a traditional territory, shows evidence of being used by Indigenous peoples, and has been continually occupied by Indigenous peoples since before the assertion of Canadian sovereignty.
>
> (Lowman and Barker, 2015: 62)

Nations must hire archeologists and other specialists to establish title with the Supreme Court of Canada. To date, Indigenous groups have amassed $1.4 billion in debt to finance this burden of proof in land cases (Lukacs, 2019: 150).

Immediately following the 1973 *Calder* decision, Inuit Tapirisat of Canada (ITC), the newly formed Inuit land claims organization, sought to establish the extent of Inuit Aboriginal title in the Arctic (Nunavut Implementation Commission, 1995: A–2.1). The initial Nunavut Constitutional Proposal, put forward in 1985, spoke to the process:

> …the fact that Inuit had been using the lands and water for as long as memory, was ignored. Today there is the bizarre situation where Inuit through land claims talks are "proving" that they are who they say they are and live where they say they live and, therefore, have some stake in the lands and resources they have always used and occupied.
>
> (Nunavut Constitutional Forum, 1985: 40).

Nonetheless, the courts were satisfied with the proof, and the land claim process continued. ITC organizer, John Amagoalik's (1976) vision of what could be negotiated was a "land-sharing proposal" (6) that would grant Inuit "real political and economic power in [our] own land" (7). ITC wanted to pursue a diversified economy

> We believe that a fair land settlement can also provide economic alternatives for Inuit, so that big-time industrial development does not have to be the only game in town. Some Inuit may want to work on the pipeline, but we would be foolhardy to look to the pipeline as a source of long-term satisfying jobs. At the present time, the only alternative to short term wage employment is welfare and the loss of pride and dignity that go with it.
>
> (ibid: 8)

ITC was not opposed to resource development: rather, it sought Inuit control over the process, the protection of land, animals, and water, and monetary benefits from resource development, seeing the NLCA as an opportunity for the "emergence of our Inuit people from colonial-style domination by others" (Amagoalik in McPherson, 2003: 145). But ITC was negotiating in a new era of Crown-Indigenous relations, the era of the comprehensive land claim – structured as a cash-for-land deal, and the Crown wanted the land. As per the Crown's goal of extinguishing Aboriginal title, the government demanded Inuit trade away their rights to the vast majority of the territory and "[i]n exchange, they receive money and small parcels of land in the form of private property, rather than in the collective way Indigenous peoples have long stewarded it" (Lukacs, 2019: 150). The Nunavut land claims process moved slowly[4] – ITC submitted a proposal to the federal government in 1976 (Amagaolik, 1976: 6) but it took until 1990 to reach an agreement-in-principle (AIP) with the Crown (McPherson, 2003). While many Inuit remained ambivalent about resource development and opposed rapid development, the Crown centred non-renewable resources in negotiations. The AIP stated settlement lands are to "promote economic self-sufficiency of Inuit through time" through "the development of non-renewable resources, including areas of known or potential mineral deposits" (Government of Canada in McPherson, 2003: 115). In short, the title to these small parcels of land – what was to become IOL – would be transferred to Inuit of Nunavut, in exchange for formally relinquishing Aboriginal title to the remaining lands (McPherson, 2003).

As such, the tradeoff for harvesting rights, ownership of culturally valued lands, and economic benefits was relenting to the government's desire to increase resource extraction. In the end, Inuit of Nunavut negotiated to retain ownership of lands with valuable minerals and decided on a portfolio that the geologist consultants hailed as economically viable. Bob Kadlun, TFN vice president at the time, said that

> Inuit are to gain ownership of many proven mineral deposits, currently under lease to third parties, some of which may be developed in the 1990s. This agreement ensures that Inuit will receive worthwhile and lasting benefits if and when mineral development occurs.
>
> (ibid: 269)

In other words, all land – even Inuit Owned Land – was pre-defined as available for resource extraction.

## Reconciling a right with a lie

While the NLCA "is often presented and celebrated as a means for strengthening Inuit and Canada's relations" (Price, 2007: 5), the state held much more power within the relationship and succeeded in securing access to resources, reconciling only the uncertainty of land ownership (ibid). The government's interest in, and now cemented control of land and resources, is central to the relationship. Even in community consultations, the Government of Canada set the frame and maintained authority (ibid). There has been a shift from blatant land theft, through the planting of flags as performative sovereignty gestures, and staking claims on Indigenous lands through free-entry, to lengthy land claims negotiations that ultimately result in the same outcomes: entrenching the colonial state apparatus (Coulthard, 2014: 7).

The NCLA is an often-celebrated example of reconciliation while in fact cements the Crown's control over land and resources. In signing an agreement underpinned by settler colonial law, invested in capitalist extractive interests, formed within a neoliberal political and economic system, the potential land uses are thereby defined within this system. Jackie Price argues:

> One cannot dispute the overarching authority of the Canadian state in this relationship. This fact is obvious, as this relationship was secured *once Inuit surrendered their [A]boriginal claim to the territory, thereby legally securing Canada's claim to Nunavut's land base*, which is supported by the individual articles in the NLCA. The majority of articles focus specifically on land and resources, expressed by descriptions of administrative processes that guide the NLCA signatories in land access and use. *In holding the legal title to the land, the Canadian state also secured its right to determine the administration of the land.* Inuit are greatly limited by this arrangement, and the majority of Inuit politicians are legally required, and politically inclined, to follow the agreement's lead. Individual Inuit interested in interacting with the issues outlined in the NLCA must depend on the governing organizations established by the NLCA to represent Inuit.
>
> (2007: 6, emphasis added)

Price goes on to say that, "land claims have not brought anything new to Indigenous communities" (ibid: 98), a sentiment echoed by James Arvaluk, ITC president in the 1970s, who dismissed the term "land claims" stating, "we are claiming nothing, we are offering to share our land with the rest of the Canadian population in return for a recognition of rights and a say in the way the land is used and developed" (in Duffy, 1988: 194). Warren Bernauer (2019) similarly argues that ongoing disputes within Inuit communities around resource development largely stem from the way the agreement incentivizes extraction as the sole revenue source for Inuit beneficiary organizations. Inuit had to negotiate within the confines of the comprehensive land claims agreement policy, which is fundamentally entrenched in a settler colonial conception of land as property.

This form of reconciliation – reconciling Crown sovereignty – will continue to fail because

> …it attempts the impossible–the reconciliation of a right with a lie. The right is the pre-existing interest Indigenous Peoples had and continue to

have in their land and the right to make decisions about their land before and after the colonizers' arrival. This includes the right to benefit from their land and decide how their lands should be used or not used....The lie is that through simply showing up and planting a flag, European nations could acquire an interest in Indigenous land and displace Indigenous laws.

(McIvor, 2021: 168)

Inuit had to learn the language and legal system of the colonial government, hire consultants to prove their use and occupation of their homeland, and spend decades in consultations in order to sit at the negotiating table. The colonial government fortified structural power imbalances in policy, ensuring non-renewable resources play a central role in the colonization of Inuit, from the surveys of the GSC to the negotiation of the NLCA. The map of IOL is often invoked to frame the story of the NLCA as a heroic act of collaboration. And so, in fact, while IOL has been sold – on national and international stages – as an important piece in Inuit self-determination, comprehensive land claims serve to extinguish Aboriginal title rights and enact dispossession through the rhetoric of reconciliation.

## Meanwhile, land claims negotiations reach Mary River

Once the AIP is signed, IOL has to be selected. Community land-identifying negotiating teams (CLINTs) meet in each hamlet between 1990 and 1992 to discuss the land they and their ancestors have inhabited for thousands of years. The teams rely on Elders' knowledge of historical land-use to select parcels of land for surface rights (McPherson, 2003), and geologists to select parcels of land for subsurface rights (ibid). Choosing the parcels is fraught as many Inuit see this trade-off as a penalty for signing the Agreement (ibid).

The Crown pegs Inuit's economic future to resource development, so negotiating Inuit Owned Land becomes high-stakes – subsurface IOL must have the potential for industrial production. At a Hall Beach negotiation, Solomon Qanatsiag pushes to include *nuluujaat,* the Mary River iron ore, in the deal as "his uncle had been the first to show iron mineralization to the whites" (McPherson, 2003: 2016). The proposal is blocked – the Canadian government refuses to grant Inuit rights to any land with existing third-party interests such as prospecting permits. This Crown strategy is designed to take all staked mineral deposits off the bargaining table. Inuit leaders consider exiting negotiations, taking the Crown's position as a violation of the spirit of the agreement-in-principle (ibid: 222). Chief negotiator Paul Quassa calls the negotiations "nothing more than a federal land-grab" (ibid: 226). But Inuit do not pull out – negotiations continue for two years and eventually, the Crown relents on the inclusion of staked minerals. *Nuluujaat* becomes IOL (ibid: 241).

## Notes

1 The 1973 supreme court ruling in *Calder et al. v. Attorney-General of British Columbia* affirmed the ongoing existence of Indigenous land ownership within the common law, regardless of acknowledgement in any treaty. The ruling is discussed at length in the following section.

2 For detailed analyses of the NLCA, see Henderson (2007), Price (2007), Duffy (1988) and Merrit (1989).

3 We use the term "Aboriginal title" here to speak specifically to a category of ownership rights within common law. In all other contexts, we use the term Indigenous, or specific names for different Indigenous nations.

4 For a full timeline of negotiations and implementation, see: Nunavut Implementation Commission (1995). *Footprints in new snow: a comprehensive report from the Nunavut Implementation Commission to the Department of Indian Affairs and Northern Development,* Government of the Northwest Territories and Nunavut Tunngavik Incorporated concerning the establishment of the Nunavut Government.

# 4 Reconciling waste

## Introduction

Conversations about waste often go something like this: we are producing too much waste! We must take more *responsibility*! We need to *educate* individuals about how much waste they are producing. A lot of people are not (properly) recycling their waste – we can do better! If only people cared more about the planet, we would solve our garbage problem!

This narrative is particularly popular in settler/colonial neoliberal capitalist states like Canada, New Zealand, the United States, Nouvelle Calédonie, and Australia. In these countries, Indigenous communities often (but certainly not always) have large volumes of waste, visible equally to indignant tourists, settler/colonial government officials, and researchers (not to mention the people living close to (or on) the waste). The academic version of the above narrative appears in refereed journal articles such as this:

> Arctic cities face unique challenges in managing their solid waste due to their relatively small size, remote location, extreme and rapidly changing climate, and boom-bust economies. Generally, Arctic residents produce more waste annually (0.62 tons per capita versus 0.3 tons per capita globally), while seeing lower rates of collection (90% versus 100% in many but not all cities) and recycling relatively little compared to other cities (11% on average versus 20% globally). To improve on existing conditions, *Arctic cities should prioritize implementing methods to reduce waste production and increase recycling.*
>
> (Burns et al., 2021: 340, our emphasis)

On the surface, research studies (as well as the odd news or social media item) appear to quite logically identify the problem (poor waste management) and its solution (improved waste management, mainly focused on household recycling). The common sense logic of these conclusions depends upon settler/colonial neoliberal capitalism, within which manufacturing and retail industries, as well as governments, intentionally frame waste as a post-consumer problem that may be successfully managed through technological solutions

DOI: 10.4324/9781003342526-5

and individual behavioural change (Hird, 2021, 2022). That is, publics are intentionally led to believe that their community's – and the global – waste problem is household waste, and that therefore the solution is greater individual responsibility for its minimization (achievable through increased recycling). As such, research studies such as the one quoted here effectively reinforce settler/colonial neoliberal capitalism.

This narrative is woven through with the ongoing settler/colonial neoliberal capitalist project that equates Indigenous with wrong (outdated, less civilized) and settler with right (progressive, necessary). Thus, settler/colonial neoliberal capitalist ideology, expressed as common-sense, is that if only Arctic communities would *modernize*, they would solve their own waste crises (aka the 'teach a man to fish' argument). As such, *assimilation to settler/colonial neoliberal capitalism equates to Indigenous self-determination.* It shifts attention away from waste as a symptom of ongoing settler/colonial neoliberal capitalism, and thus a social justice issue (ibid). We want to be clear: we are not claiming that researchers are intentionally contributing to settler/colonial neoliberal capitalism, blaming Indigenous communities for the veritable mountains of waste highly visible in, for instance, Arctic communities in Canada or Kanak communities in Nouvelle Calédonie. Researchers, government officials, and even some community groups are operating within an ideology that is sufficiently established and thriving to be repeated as 'common sense'.

Waste is a generous linguistic, symbolic, and material signifier. It is modernity's excess; progress's fallout. From Chris Jordan's photographs of plastics-ingested albatross to Jennifer Baichwal, Nicholas de Pencier, and Edward Burtynsky's cinematic illustration of a planet laid to waste by colossal engineering, garbage defines our species' legacy (Hird, 2012, 2015). Moreover, the banality of waste – as modernity's routine and unavoidable aftermath – undergirds the politics of our current human rights/environmental crisis in a particular way. Far from the international concern aroused by climate change, waste rather inauspiciously moves us towards a state whereby our only solution for dealing with the toxicity our relentless planetary depletion generates is producing permanently temporary waste deposits – from open dumps to landfills and radioactive waste storage facilities – for imagined futures to resolve (Hird, 2021; van Wyck, 2010). And while waste is largely out-of-sight and out-of-mind in affluent regions of the world (buried underground, incinerated or transported elsewhere), Indigenous communities from Canada to Australia, Nouvelle Calédonie and New Zealand, have waste that is easy to see, hard to miss, and everywhere. Canada's Arctic waste, whether from resource extraction, military buildup, or households, is a toxic symptom of settler/colonial neoliberal capitalism.

## Settler/colonialism's arctic waste

One of the critical differences between the waste visible in Indigenous communities, as well as on and in Indigenous lands and waters, and the largely invisible waste in 'modern' settler communities is the jumbling together – the sheer mixed up mess – of industry and community (municipal solid) waste. On May 20, 2014, a four-story pile of waste, known locally as the West40 in Iqaluit, Nunavut's capital and only city, spontaneously caught fire caused by bacterial metabolism of the dump's abundant organic and inorganic material (Varga, 2014). The West40 dump had spontaneously ignited several times prior to the May fire. Fires in September 2010 (which lasted for 36 days), January and December 2013, and January and March 2014 are thought to have contributed to the May 2014 fire. The colossal dump rests atop a peninsula that extends well into Nunavut's Frobisher Bay (named after British navigator, Martin Frobisher, see chapter 2). For over three months the fire burned continuously. Local residents filed numerous formal and informal complaints to the City regarding the smell of dump smoke; a Territorial health department advisory warned that children, women of childbearing years, pregnant women, the elderly, and those with respiratory issues should avoid breathing in dump smoke entirely (Department of Health, 2014); the local elementary school shut down twice due to children complaining of headaches; and several major community events were postponed, including the city's annual spring clean-up. Iqualit's infamous West40 dump is one of the several open waste sites located near or within the City of Iqaluit.

In January 2013, a 1995 map of the city's contaminated waste sites resurfaced in the local Nunavut newspaper. Most (if not all) of these sites are left over from federal government military and resource development initiatives. And the municipal solid waste openly dumped in Arctic communities is a small fraction of the resource extraction industries' (and its attendant military) waste portfolio. The Canol pipeline project, for instance, moved some 40,000 military personnel and civilian workers to the North in 1942 in order to secure a pipeline from Norman Wells, Northwest Territories to Whitehorse, Yukon. Operational for just one year, the pipeline closed because more oil was spilled on the land than transported (Perić, 2015). This military-industrial enterprise abandoned hundreds of trucks, graders, and construction equipment, as well as some 60,476 barrels of oil in the pipe, and some 108,857 barrels that are presumed to have spilled into the landscape (Up Here, 2014). Constructed in 1942 in the wake of the attack on Pearl Harbour, the Alaskan Highway would eventually connect the contiguous United States to Alaska through Canada's British Columbia and Yukon. Although celebrated for taking less than a year to build, the highway was mired with technological problems caused by permafrost – challenges that still cause re-routing. The project moved thousands of tons of construction equipment North, and the work crews dubbed the road the 'oil can highway' because of the sheer number of oil cans and fuel drums they discarded along the road. Amongst its other waste by-products, the Athabasca tar sands processing dumps 480 million gallons of contaminated toxic water into 'tailing lakes' *per day* (Huseman and Short, 2012: 221).

The Arctic's waste, moreover, has also accumulated "ex-orbitantly" (Clark, 2005): in January 1978, the Soviet Satellite Cosmos 954 exploded through the atmosphere over the Northwest Territories, spreading some sixty-five kilograms of fissionable uranium-235 over an area of 124,000 square kilometres (Heaps, 1978), providing another dramatic illustration – like the plastics and POPs drifting northwards and accumulating in the Arctic – that waste does not respect national boundaries. Moreover, there are approximately (no one knows the exact figure) 27,000 abandoned or "orphaned" mines in Canada, most of which are in Canada's northern regions. The Giant Mine, located on the Ingraham Trail close to Yellowknife, was abandoned in 2005, leaving some 100 on-site buildings, eight open pits, and contaminated soils and waste rock around the mine, including some 237,000 tons of arsenic trioxide dust (Sandlos and Keeling, 2012). There are over 10,000 orphaned oil and gas wells in Alberta alone (Orphan Well Association, 2023).

Persistent Organic Pollutants (POPs) from all over the world end up in polar regions through what scientists term the Grasshopper Effect. Many POPs are industrial waste by-products that are transported to the Arctic via air currents from southern communities. Contaminants evaporate in warm temperatures and condense in cold climates where they accumulate on the land and in country food. As a result, women who eat country food have higher contaminant loads in their breast milk than those who do not (Kafarowski, 2004; see also Cone, 2005). Canadian law regulates the disposal of sewage and greywater at sea except for the Arctic Ocean where "any ship and any person on a ship may deposit in the arctic waters such sewage as may be generated" (*Arctic Shipping Pollution Prevention Regulations*, C.R.C., c. 353, s. 28). The thousands of vessels travelling the Arctic since 1990 are mainly tourism, research, and federal government military support vessels (Pizzolato et al., 2014). A recent study reveals that concentrations of microplastics (plastics debris that are less than 5mm in diameter) in high Arctic sea ice are over two orders of magnitude greater than what is found in all other ocean surface waters, including the so-called Great Pacific Garbage Patch (Obbard et al., 2014) and concludes that the Arctic is a "global sink" (ibid, 318) for microplastic debris.

And the Highway of the Atom (van Wyck, 2010) refers to a route travelled by uranium mined by Sahtú Dene on the shores of Great Bear Lake, over land to Port Hope and then to the United States and the Manhattan Project, where it was eventually dropped on Hiroshima and Nagasaki during World War II. In the 1930s and the 1940s, the Sahtú Dene were employed by the Eldorado Gold Mines corporation to mine uranium ore without knowing of its effect on their health and their environment (tons of radium tailings dumped into the lake, and many kilometres of ground), living generations later with its after effects: depression, addiction, cancers, mutating (and dying) flora and fauna.

## Pagans to waste, lands to save

As the previous discussion about the Doctrine of Discovery reveals, contemporary drives towards Arctic resource exploitation have a long theological and legal fuse. Judeo-Christian ideology shaped not just ownership regimes and dispossession, but beliefs about the appropriate uses for land. Having either saved, subdued, and enslaved pagan souls for God's work or otherwise saved these souls from the devil's clutches by killing their human bodies, Judeo-Christian orthodoxy extended god's will to land-use imperatives (Saul, 2008). In Old and Middle English, 'waste' referred generally to the environment, and more specifically to uninhabitable (to Europeans) land. In the 1200s, the Anglo-French word for waste meant 'desolate regions' and in Old North French it referred to 'damage, destruction, wasteland, or moor'. By c.1300, the Old English word 'waste' meant 'a desert, a wilderness' from the Latin 'empty, desolate, waste'. Into the 1600s, waste still referred to land that was 'unfit for use' (ibid). Land which appeared so desolate, and inhospitable was synonymous with wilderness. Wilderness, in short, was wasted land: a waste/land.[1]

Within Judeo-Christian morality, wastelands are not only places of desolation and hostility, but also carry a certain obligation – these are places that may be redeemed through effort, hard work, and conviction. In his *Second Treatise of Government*, John Locke wrote:

> God, when he [sic] gave the world in common to all mankind [sic], commanded man also to labour, and the penury of his condition required it of him. God and his reason commanded him to subdue the earth, i.e. improve it for the benefit of life, and therein lay out something upon it that was his own, his labour.
>
> (1869/2011: section 25, Chapter 5)

The way to redeem idle land is to transform it – through 'Man's' labour – into usable, useful, and cultivated land. There needs, in other words, to be a mark on the land. Land not marked by 'Man' is land un-remarkable, unused, and unusable; again, a waste. Waste, as John Scanlan moreover reminds us, is about indeterminateness: "the references to places or things that belong to neither one person nor another, its [waste] being the original condition of nature's chaos" (2005: 25, our emphasis; see also Hird, 2012). Wasted and unused land is therefore *without sovereignty*. Scanlan goes on to point out that, from this European Judeo-Christian perspective, a wasteland is effectively witness to human failure to work the land, to make it usable, and to tame nature and bring it under 'Man's' dominion. In this sense, Scanlan argues, waste and its opposite – utility and value – is "a way of knowing the material world" (ibid: 132). Waste lands are, by definition, places beyond European Judeo-Christian comprehension.

Notwithstanding prospector and settlers' dependence on Inuit for survival, navigation, hunting, and labour (Brody, 2000; Qikiqtani Inuit Association, 2010; Paine, 1977; Wachowich, 1994), many historical accounts describe Inuit as surviving in the Arctic before colonization. These accounts describe Inuit as (barely) sustaining themselves in such an inhospitable wasteland despite their primitive status and lack of technology. Inuit were not characterized as working the land in a useful Judeo-Christian fashion, which meant planting, growing, and harvesting crops. Indeed, Inuit were sometimes regarded as children in need of instruction and governance. Note, for instance, Fridtjof Nansen's preface to Diamond Jenness's *The People of the Twilight*, written in 1959:

> One cannot read this charming narrative without getting a deep sympathy for these simple, unsophisticated children of the twilight … a charming people of happy children, not yet stung by the burden of our culture, not burdened by the intricate problems and the acid dissatisfaction of our society.
>
> (in Jenness, 1959: v)

Whilst Inuit *had* already been "stung" by colonization by this time, it is clear that from this perspective, hunter-gatherer ways of living with the land seemed not only primitive, but also idle: making no mark, utility, or command of the land rendered it a wasteland and its people in need of stewardship and proper governance (Brody, 2000).

And lest this Judeo-Christian configuration of unused (read uncolonized) land be insufficient, the ideology extends the concept of waste to human beings. The longstanding association of waste, dirt, and disease with racialized and colonized peoples as a justification for practices of subjugation offers insights into waste as a cultural signifier with consequences from social stigmatization to excommunication and death (see Douglas, [1966] 2007; Kristeva, 1982). The line between resourceful and dirty was (and is) largely dictated by particular Judeo-Christian configurations about cleanliness and waste. Whereas prior to colonization, Inuit lived largely as extended family units that moved across land, ice, and water according to carefully monitored hunting and gathering seasons, the profound shift that settler colonialism caused to Inuit way of life towards wage labour and a market-based economy was reinforced by several directed government initiatives. Examining the development of Iqaluit, Nunavut's capital, Matthew Farish and P. Whitney Lackenbauer note that by the mid-1950s, Euro-Canadian bureaucrats had taken a "high modernist" approach to economic and political development in the Arctic. The explicit goal was to build "a nation in the northern half of this continent truly patterned on our [southern] way of life" (2009: 520). More than this, the North American Arctic was meant to become a "safe space for development projects" (ibid). As more and more Inuit were assimilated into the capitalist market economy, Inuit across Nunavut began to rent govern-ment subsidized housing. These houses were often described as unfit for the climate, and most relied on electricity for heating that was turned off if tenants did not make their rent payments. All government employees were enjoined to "assist" Inuit people's transition to civilization by "insist[ing] upon the main-tenance of cleanliness and sanitation amongst the Eskimo [sic] employees and their famil[ies]" (Lackenbauer and Shackleton, 2012: 10). By 1960, for example, scavenging for household materials was banned in Resolute Bay. Canadian government reports from the mid-twentieth century discussed the difficulty Inuit had in adapting to Euro-Canadian standards of waste manage-ment. Similar to American colonialists in the Philippines, who, as Warwick Anderson points out, quite literally examined slides of Indigenous people's faeces, Canadian federal government employees were sent to inspect the cleanliness of Inuit houses. It was noted by government officials that Inuit women's housekeeping "lacks organization". Federal government officials recorded Inuit diet ("almost all the food was bought from the store"), patterns of food preparation ("soups are heated but do not always have water added to them"), shopping ("men make most of the purchases"), and cleanliness ("toilet bowls are allowed to fill before they are removed ... washing clothes is still a problem in many homes"). In the late 1960s, adult education classes were provided to Inuit women whose housekeeping did not "measure up to the standards set by white women".

As Marie Lathers notes, "management of the abject" (i.e., of faeces, dirt, or waste) was central to the American (and we would argue global) colonial project of the early twentieth century. The particularities of this project devel-oped through a discourse of "excremental colonialism" wherein the "brown person" became disempowered (and dehumanized) through their associa-tion with the abject. Indeed, one government official noted with disgust that when Inuit began wearing Euro-Canadian cotton materials, the clothing was worn "until ... it fairly rots off". Here, as Anderson puts it, waste was used to delineate "the polar opposites of white and brown, retentive and promiscu-ous, imperforate and open, pure and polluting, civilized and infantile". Only fitting, then, that – according to colonizers – naturally unclean, uncivilized, and dirty Inuit enter the capitalist wage labour system as maids, cleaners, launders, and waste collection and disposal workers. As we write this chap-ter, Manitoba Keewatinowi Okimakanak and Long Plain First Nation lead-ers are calling for a search of the Prairie Green landfill, where the remains of Marcedes Myran, Morgan Harris, and Mashkode Bizhiki'ikwe (named by community members because they do not know who she is) are suspected to have been dumped by their killer. After city officials refused the request, and public outcry ensued, the federal government is now promising to fund the landfill excavation feasibility study (The Canadian Press, 2023). In July 2023, the Manitoba government declared that it would not search the landfill for the remains of Harris and Myran. Protestors blocked the road to the landfill in protest, and the blockade has now been taken down. Protests continue outside the Canadian Museum for Human Rights. Rebecca Contois's body, also Indigenous and also murdered, has already been found to have been partially dumped in a garbage bin and at the Brady Road landfill. As Nicole Murdock notes:

> In Canada, Indigenous women, girls and two-spirit people are intentionally targeted and disproportionately subjected to violence. We represent 28 percent of women who are murdered, despite making up only four per cent of the population in Canada. We are 12 times more likely to be murdered or go missing than non-Indigenous women.

(ibid: np)

Commenting on the city's original refusal to search for the Indigenous women's bodies, Joyce Jonathan Crone asks 'Why are we, Indigenous women, disposable garbage?' (2022: np).

## Reconciling waste

The research quoted at the beginning of this chapter focuses on household waste in Indigenous communities. Waste studies research amply documents that extraction, manufacturing, military, and other industrial forms of waste (such as construction) accounts for, by orders of magnitude, most (by volume and often toxicity) waste (Arboleda, 2020; Hird, 2021, 2022; Lepawsky, 2018; Liboiron and Lepawsky, 2022). This is the case across Canada, and even more so in remote regions where resource extraction occurs. The misdirected focus is common to all regions of Canada and equally applies to metropolitan cities as it does to rural communities. For neoliberal capitalism to (continue to) succeed, the focus on household waste is critical because it draws attention away from the human health and environmental consequences of capitalism's aftermath, and magnifies both neoliberalism (individual responsibility) and the capitalism (through the profit-driven waste management industry and techno-fixes).

And so, Iqaluit's ongoing West40 fires are characterized as a problem of households producing too much waste and of municipal responsibility to better manage this form of waste through modern technologies. Official reports de-emphasize (or do not mention at all) the fact that the dump is a result of successive Crown governments, industries and military settlement, and ongoing buildup. Or that Iqaluit's household waste is a consequence of the profound shift to wage labour, forced settlements, and dependence on highly packaged (and extraordinarily expensive) store-bought food rather than traditional food harvesting. Researchers' formulaic recommendation that remote Indigenous communities should recycle belies the reality that there is no profit (and, indeed, considerable cost and negative environmental impacts) in transporting materials to southern recycling processing centres (Hird, 2021). Like waste management, recycling is a capitalist profit-driven enterprise, however successfully recycling companies disguise it as a social and environmental good. Recycling serves double-duty as well, inasmuch as it falsely reifies the individual (neoliberalism) as the solution to the waste crisis. Thus, in terms of waste, reconciliation operates well with colonial governments in 'encouraging' Indigenous communities to 'take responsibility' in managing the waste in their territory. Managing, here, refers to adopting 'modern' technologies such as engineered landfills and incinerators, which bring enormous profits to waste management companies. Managing also means educational programs designed to increase individuals' adoption of, and adaptation to, these technologies – in short, the individual behavioural change that is central to neoliberal principles.

Critically, modernizing also means embracing increased resource extraction. Canada has a 'dig now, pay later' resource extraction history. As Anne Dance et al. note, "...politicians, bureaucrats, and industry representatives often differentiate between two periods of Canadian mining: an earlier era of regulatory laxness and limited reclamation, and its modern, enlightened counterpart from the 1980s onwards" (2022: 197). This earlier period allowed companies and the military to abandon thousands of mines and other resource extraction and security projects (such as the Distant Early Warning (DEW) Line) across Canada, with little or no consequences to industry, and profound consequences to the land, water, and local peoples. The outrageousness of it all is not only that the DEW Line stations were redundant before they were operational, or that Canadian taxpayers footed the bill for this largely American operation, or that less than half of these radar stations have undergone any remediation. It is that the DEW Line is one of many waste sites created in the name of national security, (Canadian) sovereignty, and capitalist competition (staking 'our' claim on oil, gas, and mineral deposits before the next country does) with the now-ubiquitous 'local labour opportunities' thrown in as a kind of stool-softener (step right up, join us today, and you join our ever-expanding settler/colonial capitalism). It is that Indigenous lands and waters are routinely exploited and then abandoned by industry and government. Nothing is hidden because Indigenous peoples live, hunt, gather, and move on this land and these waters. Nothing is sequestered away because there is no 'away'.

The contemporary Jericho Diamond Mine, Faro Mine, and Giant Mine disasters – mines abandoned to Crown responsibility at a cost of millions to taxpayers, environmental devastation, and profound local community including long-term health and socio-economic issues – attest to the fact that contemporary resource extraction follows in much the same footsteps as it always has. Numerous Indigenous communities, organizations, and legal forces, as well as various national and territorial bodies such as the National Orphaned/Abandoned Mines Initiative (NOAMI), the Federal Contaminated Sites Inventory (FCAI), and the Department of Natural Resources document contaminated mining waste sites across Canada. MiningWatch Canada, other NGOs, and an increasing number of researchers (see, for example, Kuyek, 2019; Beckett, 2021) report the environmental, human health, and social justice costs that resource extraction exact. The focus on mining site remediation demonstrates that the federal government and resource extraction industry interests strongly intersect in securing continued and, as unfettered as possible access, to oil, gas, and minerals.

As Dance et al. (2022) point out, the Crown emphasizes remediation. In other words, there is no question of decreasing resource extraction: reports, committee meetings, and debates turn on how much remediation is necessary, how much it is going to cost, and who is going to pay for it. Remediation (variously known as rehabilitation, reclamation, or cleanup) suggests that resource extraction sites can be physically returned to their pre-construction condition. But this is far from the case. Remediation means rendering land reusable for capital profit. Remediation is how we end up with ski hills made from closed landfills, and recreational parks made from closed munitions factories (Krupar, 2013).

Let's take, for instance, the material excess that the United States and Canadian militaries, and private corporations, Western Electric Corporation and Bell Technologies, created when they built 63 DEW Line stations across Alaska, Nunavut, Greenland, and Iceland: waste oil, PCB transformers/capacitors, asbestos, sewage, lead-based paints, radioactive tubes, scrap metal, radar components, fuel barrels, lime, antifreeze, wood, aviation fuel, sulphamic acid, cathode ray tubes and screens, filtron tubes, oscillators, meters, copper wire, transmission fluid, 1-1-1-trichloroethane, PBX telephone equipment, mercury vapour rectifier tubes, paint thinners, batteries, chlorinated hydrocarbons, corrosion inhibitors, lye, corrosives, paper, plastic, solvents, dynamite, RF interference filters, generators, scopes, vehicles, and rubber fuel bladders (Environmental Sciences Group and UMA Engineering Ltd. 1995). Over 30 tons of polychlorinated biphenyls (PCBs) were found up to 15 km away from various sites. The colossal waste produced during the construction of the (never operational) DEW Line, detailed at the beginning of this chapter, illustrates the limits of remediation. Discussing the lengthy assessment of the feasibility of remediating the DEW Line sites, the Environmental Sciences Group (ESG) report concedes, "The Protocol recognizes that this restoration will not return the environment to a pristine state, but will at least remove most barriers to long-term natural reclamation" (1993: 30). As Heather Ducharme (2004) observes, whether the terms "cleanup" or "remediation" are used, both actually involve further material development of landfills and burns. Even the assessment process has involved further environmental disturbance: the "environmental sampling to survey the damage has involved some 4,000 soil/sediment/water, 1,600 plant, and 500 marine/animal tissue samples" (ibid, 15). Moreover, much of the material brought to the Arctic has – if it is below the protocol's threshold for contamination – been left there. And the vast quantities of material (soil, barrels, and so on) that are so contaminated that they must be removed to the South are then not cleaned up but rather buried in southern landfills or incinerated, a process that produces highly toxic fly ash that must then be stored in specially designed facilities (Rowe, 2012).

At Resolution Island alone, which Scott Mitchell (DIAND director of the contaminated sites remediation) estimates cost a third of the total DEW Line remediation expense, scientists found that over 8,000 kg of pure PCBs (called Aroclor 1260) had been abandoned after the site closed (Kalinovich et al., 2008). These PCBs had migrated through a valley, descended cliffs, and moved into Frobisher Bay, from which local Inuit fish. The fuel and oil that had also been openly dumped had forged a path for the PCBs, facilitating their migration over the land and into the sea. Describing the scene scientists found at Resolution Island, Canadian hazardous waste specialist Robert Eno said: "Looking at what you'd found there, you'd think that Americans took big hoses and sprayed PCB liquid all over the site" (in Capozza, 2002: 15). PCBs are a known carcinogen, increasing the incidence of cancer, bacterial infections, liver lesions, and genetic defects with exposure. PCBs have shown up in polar bears, foxes, voles, trout, and other country food upon which Inuit depend (Danon-Schaffer, 2015). This site alone cost $64.75 million to remediate and involved some 595 people in the operation (Kalinovich et al., 2008). Oil spills in Hooper Bay, Cape Romanzof, and Point Hope amount to some 80,000 gallons (303 m3) of petroleum leaked into the environment.

Some of the barrels contained petroleum products (fuel, lubricants); antifreeze (glycols); degreasers (halogenated aliphatics); and cadmium, chromium, lead, and chlorine, as well as the staggering amounts of PCBs. But scientists found the highest levels of PCBs at the Sarcpa Lake site, as well as solvents, mercury, and petroleum products; buildings and other infrastructure; and abandoned barrels, sewage, and other debris (Poland, Mitchell, and Rutter, 2001). At the Iqaluit and other DEW Line and Pinetree sites, scientists had to remove not only the buildings, which had asbestos clad piping, but also thousands of barrels abandoned from the DEW Line project, and those left on the site from more recent industrial activities. Waste remediation in the Arctic often requires physically moving contaminated waste to southern disposal facilities, which are completely absent in the Arctic due to their very high associated costs, and physical challenges such as permafrost (see, for instance, Thomassin-Lacroix, 2015). At the Iqaluit site, not only did the buildings require demolishing, but also the concrete foundations had to be removed and shipped South for disposal – according to the DEW Line Cleanup (DLCU) Protocol (2005) – because the PCBs had entirely penetrated the concrete to 50 to 70 cm (the DLCU Protocol requires PCBs at more than 50 ppm to be shipped to a licensed disposal facility). The PCB-contaminated drums found at the DEW Line site in Iqaluit had to be flown from Iqaluit to Yellowknife, and then land-transported to a PCB incineration facility in southern

Canada (Poland, Mitchell, and Rutter 2001). Some further 307 meters of soil contaminated at the DCC Tier II level (5–50 ppm) was placed in specially designed fabric boxes and shipped to a waste disposal site near Montréal. Engineers had the extra challenge of designing viable landfills that could be excavated in hard rock and permafrost. Technologies used in the South such as incineration, thermal desorption, and solvent extraction prove to be unviable in the North as they are too expensive, require very large amounts of fuel (which would need to be shipped North), produce residues that must be shipped South for disposal, or incompletely deal with the contamination. Describing the Resolution Island cleanup, scientists noted the unique challenges of waste remediation in the North: "The magnitude of the PCB contamination is very large, the terrain mountainous, the site extremely remote, the climate is particularly harsh and polar bears are regular visitors" (Poland, Mitchell, and Rutter, 2001: 96).

Remediation is also the current name of the reconciliation game for another critical reason: the dramatic increase in demand for northern natural resources. Over the past 20 years, this demand has only intensified with climate change and its indeterminacies making these resources more accessible by way of, for instance, opening up the Northwest Passage to year-round shipping (Hird, 2021; Southcott, 2012). Although the exact industrial prospects are unknown, according to then Aboriginal Affairs and Northern Development Canada, the North contains about 25% of Canada's discovered recoverable crude oil and natural gas, and about 40% of Canada's projected future discoveries (Government of Canada, 2010). Foreign companies such as British Petroleum are making enormous bids for exploration rights, and countries such as China and India are seeking non-Arctic observer status at the Arctic Council (Griffiths, Huebert, and Lackenbauer, 2011). Much depends on a number of factors that remain uncertain at this time: what proportion of what resources (oil, gas, gas hydrates, minerals, and so on) will be uncovered, at what costs, and with what developed technology, and in what market climate? These unavoidable uncertainties also mean uncertainties in the amounts and kinds of waste production as a result of this industrial and military push in the Arctic. In simple terms, more people and equipment moving temporarily from South to North, and much more drilling and extraction, inevitably means more waste. And although Lackenbauer and Farish stop short of identifying the Arctic as a so-called sacrifice area, they are clear about the devastating impacts of the military/industrial presence in the Arctic. Referring to the Arctic, they observe:

> These military mega-projects radically transformed the human and physical geography of the North. Bulldozers tore permafrost off the ground disrupting ecosystems and creating impassable quagmires. Forest fires, logging, over-hunting, and over-fishing depleted resources in the region.

Arriving workers brought diseases from measles and VD, which devastated Indigenous populations.

> (2007: 925. See also Kafarowski, 2004;
> Sandlos and Keeling, 2012)

As metals, oil, gas, fracking, and other industries increasingly turn their collective extractive gazes northwards, Indigenous communities have few resources to effectively mitigate the fallout accumulation, much less refuse.

## Conclusions

Certainly, the securities requirement of resource extraction companies *could* be better calculated to reflect the enormous costs of extraction site aftercare, more consistently collected and more strongly enforced. The environmental assessment that companies are now required to undertake *could*, likewise, more accurately and strongly represent and prioritize local community and environment concerns. It *could* emphasize long-term (centuries to millennia) rather than short-term (decades) impacts. Resource extraction companies' community engagement requirement *could* be made to include historical and contemporary settler colonialism, social justice and inequity concerns, rather than short-term job prospects. Canada *could* get rid of the free entry system that protects companies from prosecution as they prospect on private property.

These changes, as with calls for stricter remediation policies and practices, *could*, as Caitlyn Beckett argues, be put to service as "…an anticolonial mechanism to (re)structure, or (re)mediate, relationships with both land and people" (2021: 1389). As – by definition – remediation is after-the-fact of environmental devastation, whatever revisions to it are made, they are made within settler/colonial neoliberal capitalism. Remediation, as a cornerstone of reconciliation, works well with forms of liberal environmentalism

> Liberal environmentalism is so compatible with contemporary material and cultural currency that it implicitly supports the very things that it should be criticizing. Its technocratic, scientist, and even economistic character gives credence to a society that measures the quality of life fundamentally in terms of economic growth, control over nature, and the maximization of sheer efficiency in everything we do. By working to show that environmental protection need not compromise these maxims, liberal environmentalism fails to raise deeper issues that more fundamentally engage the dynamics of environmental degradation.
>
> (Wapner, 1996: 21–2)

And so, all of these 'coulds' remain unrealized potentialities: they are part of a reckoning's tool-kit; not reconciliation. At this time of writing, Alberta's

Premier, Danielle Smith, is proposing the RStar program, through which extraction industries will, according to Peter Guthrie, Smith's newly appointed energy minister "incentivize the cleanup and reclamation of wells, and in doing so, it creates a royalty credit for future drilling" (in May, 2022: np). In a complete reversal of the polluter-pays principle, this program will pay resource extractive industry companies money to clean up the waste that they are already, by law, responsible for. The money will come from taxpayers, and it will promote more extractive industry activity, which will create more waste.

## Meanwhile, *Nuluujaat* becomes Deposit One

In 2006, decades after Murray Watts staked his claim, iron ore prices rise dramatically, making Mary River ore extraction profitable (isuma.tv, nd). The ore is on Inuit Owned Land (IOL), so Baffinland must establish an Inuit Impact Benefit Agreement, which promises royalties and jobs to the surrounding communities (Sinclair, 2017: 14). Mining operations begin in 2014, and *Nuluujaat* gets a new name: Deposit One. These promises are not kept. Inuit employment at the mine remains low – 21% in 2014, dropping to 17% in 2015 (ibid: 24). Royalty payments are lower than promised – the regional Inuit organization enters arbitration with Baffinland in 2017 (Nunatsiaq, 2017). And just two years after operations begin, the Nunavut Impact Review Board expresses concern over environmental management at the site – caches of waste have built up, monitoring for sulphur dioxide emissions and terrestrial species has ceased, and dust levels are higher than anticipated (Nunatsiaq, 2016). Concerns from the community level and from environmental and Inuit organizations rack up, but Baffinland pushes forward: in 2017 the company applies to expand operations with a plan for Phase 2 (Bell, 2017).

## Note

1 As William Cronon details, the Bible is replete with references to wilderness as wasteland, "places on the margins of civilization where it is all too easy to lose oneself in moral confusion and despair" (1996, 8). Wilderness is where Moses wandered with his people for forty years, nearly forsaking god and resorting to idol worship. And it is in wilderness that Jesus Christ endured forty days and was tempted by the devil. Adam and Eve were cast out of Eden to wilderness, where they and their descendants endured pain, suffering, and hardship. Land in "its raw state", writes Cronon, "had little or nothing to offer civilized men and women" (1996: 9).

# Conclusions
## Reckoning

### Introduction

*Extracting Reconciliation*'s bottom line is this: in its current rendering, reconciliation is not working. Or more precisely, it *is* working in service of those settler colonial neoliberal capitalist structures and practices that keep Indigenous lands and waters open for (resource extraction) business. As we have detailed in this book, the first wave of settler colonization planted reconciliation's roots in the land, air, and water (now called Canada) long ago. Each successive wave of settler colonialism added to, and complexified, Crown laws, regulations, policies, and practices regarding the 'Indian problem'. Today, the reconciliation's front-stage focuses on individual actions. Behind the scenes, levels of government in line-step with industry are feverishly devising all means and ways to secure resource extraction access, including open violence. No surprise, then, that numerous scholars, activists, and members of the public lament the slow pace of reconciliation: intentionally slow and steady wins the modern settler colonial neoliberal capitalist race.

### The front stage: Individuals, apologies and trying to change the system from within

As this book has shown, successive governments and companies emphasize reconciliation as individual action. Entirely predictable within reconciliation – but with nevertheless intense speculation and media coverage – in 2022, Pope Francis issued an apology for the Catholic Church's organization and participation in the residential school system, as well as its coverup (which continues today: the Vatican refuses to release documents that may well provide critical information). He followed on the heels of Justin Trudeau's apology on behalf of all Canadians the year before, after the unmarked graves of 751 children were found on residential school grounds in Saskatchewan. In his speech, Trudeau remarked that Canadians were "horrified and ashamed" of what happened (in Gilmore, 2021: np).

DOI: 10.4324/9781003342526-6

This reconciliation narrative promises not simply an acknowledgement of the past, but at least to some degree, its cleansing as well: it assuages both White guilt and fragility. Equally, the reconciliation narrative suggests a sum-of-its-parts solution. Millions of settlers perhaps making individual acknowledgements *of the past* by adding land acknowledgments to their community organization presentations, perhaps wearing orange T-shirts on designated days, perhaps reading the TRC's Executive Summary, perhaps visiting a local reservation, perhaps voting for governments that represent this acknowledgment – perhaps a lot of other things. Perhaps some individuals doing *all* of these things. Perhaps *all* individuals doing *all* of these things.

We are not arguing that any of these individual actions are either inadequate or wrong. It's actually worse. Unless these individual actions are the on-ramp to systemic government and industry change, then even the sum of these individual actions are tools in service to the Crown. They occupy well-meaning individuals – they keep us busy – and divert energy and attention away from land and water sovereignty: "performative reconciliation can heighten a sense that things are changing, and expectations that things will continue to change. It looks good. It shows well. It is politically correct" (Wilson-Raybould, 2023: 293). At best, as individual settlers, we may occupy ourselves with the questions of how to be effective allies to Indigenous peoples. And several Indigenous leaders, activists, and scholars are graciously and generously detailing – over and over again, at apparent *infinitem* over generations – what individual-level allyship means. For instance, in *True Reconciliation: How to Be a Force for Change* (2023), Jody Wilson-Raybould addresses reconciliation's achilles heel head-on. Wilson-Raybould distinguishes between what she calls Track 1 and Track 2 lines of reconciliation. Track 1 consists of "closing the gap on socio-economic issues - such as ensuring clean drinking water and access to quality education, and addressing issues of children and family and the unacceptable rate of kids in care" (2023: 238). Track 2 "is the foundation and transformational piece of rights recognition" and includes "supporting Indigenous nations in rebuilding their governing systems and implementing their right of self-government, including so that they can lead and hold the responsibility and authority to fix the challenges of Track 1" (ibid: 229). What Wilson-Raybould calls Track 2, we call reckoning. We use this term for precisely the reasons Canada's former Attorney General does: "Seeking to address Track 1…without tackling Track 2 in any coherent or meaningful way, will not work. It cannot work. It will never work" (ibid: 234). Indeed, Wilson-Raybould succinctly demonstrates that the ongoing systematic and purposeful failure to address Track 2 (reckoning) rights "is at the foundation of the urgent social and economic crises we see today (Track 1)" (ibid: 236). The Crown's refusal to reckon with Indigenous nations' land titles and rights, in other words, causes the very crises (unsafe drinking water and so on) that reconciliation is supposed to solve.

Within 'the academy', we do not need to imagine what reconciliation looks like: this book joins other critiques of the failures of our current reconciliation path. We might instead consider what reckoning with Indigenous rights (taking action on Wilson-Raybould's Tracks 1 and 2) would look like. Over generations, a university builds an authentic relationship with the Nation or Nations whose land it occupies. This authentic relationship, built up over generations, has been, and continues to be, difficult at times. Hard truths must be learned and understood, and the visitors on Indigenous lands take this learning and understanding seriously. Pretendians are not a concern because Indigenous governance is integral to the university. This is so because the university does not blend, add, incorporate, or otherwise assimilate Indigenous worldviews, knowledges, and practices within the hegemonic settler colonial neoliberal capitalist system. The members of the university, from staff and faculty to administrators and students, make symbolic performative acts of reconciliation through email land acknowledgments, orange T-shirt days, changing building names, and so on. And the university knows that for any of these symbolic performative acts to have meaning, it must take seriously its responsibility to reckon with ongoing settler colonial neoliberal capitalism in the form of, for instance, rent payments to the Nation(s), which recognizes the inherent right to Indigenous self-determination, or dismantling itself if its tenure as uninvited guests has outworn its welcome. Researchers at the university take seriously the incommensurabilities as well as affinities and their implications for all fields of study, from genetics to posthumanisms.

Settler researchers within and outside of the academy take up work that is not oriented towards reconciliation (Tuck and Yang, 2012). Fields of study such as posthumanisms converse with their settler colonial (and all of its inherent racism and sexism) foundations to reckon with, rather than reconcile, Indigenous world views and knowledges. Settler researchers recognize that to imagine a conceptual bridge between fields of study (posthumanisms, biology, geology, mathematics, for instance) and Indigenous ontologies is to misunderstand how ontologies are generated and hold traction, and to erase the violence of (in)humanist thought. It is equally to evade the physical spaces where posthumanisms research and practices emerge and flourish, such as universities.

## The back stage: Reconciliation's afterlife

The contaminating wastes that resource extraction leaves in its wake cannot be meaningfully resolved through reconciliation: those neoliberal capitalist management strategies whose ultimate aim is to keep lands and waters available for further, intensified, resource extraction (i.e. remediation). Resource extraction's wastes – tailings ponds, mental health issues, toxic soil, unemployment, contaminated drinking water, food insecurity, abandoned infrastructure, overcrowded housing, and more besides – merit a response beyond reconciliation's capacities. When waste is on the agenda, reconciliation tends to focus on communities' household waste (for which individuals are held responsible rather than the settler colonial system that tethers communities to over-packaged food from the south), individual solutions such as recycling, and techno-fixes such as waste management technologies, which employ more southern experts and increase southern waste management companies' profits – all within the colonial discourse of modern civilization.

As Chapter 4 detailed, as much as global capitalism is investing in renewable energy, it remains heavily invested in oil and gas energy, as well as the (rare earth) minerals required for electronics (electric vehicles and so on). As global resources decrease, resource extraction increases in a context of more scarcity, more competition, and more aggression and violence (to wit: the federal government's extension of the Royal Canadian Mounted Police's Anti-terrorism' K-Division Integrated National Security Enforcement Team in 2012 to protect the oil industry from attacks "against extremists", in this case the Yinka Dene Alliance. See Preston, 2013: 43). In this global political and economic environment, reconciliation proves anemic: some changes are made; there is some clean-up. And then we're good to go: keep extracting, keep the process going, make it 'sustainable' within settler colonial neoliberal capitalist terms. Christopher Wright and Daniel Nyberg sum up: "…as we continue to shamble towards a tipping point from which any meaningful return will be utterly impossible, a familiar message rings out from the corporate world: 'business as usual'" (2015: 1).

For this reason, Indigenous communities and their allies emphasize sovereignty and/or self-determination in new resource extraction projects, and perpetual care rather than remediation in these projects' aftermath (Kuyek, 2018). As Caitlynn Beckett notes:

> Seemingly, by using the term remediation (rather than restoration, reclamation or rehabilitation), governments and industry limit the narrative to one of containment, management and improvement (Dillon, 2014; Nunn, 2018). However, the practices of restoration, reclamation and remediation all share a narrative posited on the unproblematic return or recreation of an ideal or controlled environment, which occludes ongoing environmental injustices and focuses on technical fixes. Strategies for addressing environmental injustices and structures of colonialism through these clean-up practices are typically overlooked or understated in definitions of restoration, reclamation and remediation.
>
> (2021: 1392)

Neoliberal capitalism has, of course, inevitably leached into Indigenous communities, as William Carroll and J.P. Sapinski note (2018). Some communities negotiate (with more, less, or no enthusiasm) resource extraction industry projects (Atleo, 2021). Settler colonialism, capitalism, and neoliberalism have violently set the parameters: so how could it be otherwise? And some Indigenous communities fight it out alone or with allies. This, as Tom Flanagan (conservative political activist and advisor to Stephen Harper) wrote in his Resource Industries and Security Issues in Northern Alberta report for the Canadian Defense and Foreign Affairs Institute – is an actual – yet still uncommon – threat to settler colonial capitalism:

> If two or more of the five categories of people described above – saboteurs, eco-terrorists, mainstream environmentalists, Treaty 8 First Nations, and Métis – came together in a single movement, they could become a serious obstacle to development, given that innumerable roads, pipelines, and physical installations are widely spread across the huge, thinly settled, lightly policed territory of northern Alberta and adjacent areas of British Columbia and Saskatchewan. But such a convergent movement is unlikely to emerge, because of pronounced differences of interest and lifestyle among the potential opponents of development.
>
> (in Preston, 2013: 52)

Globally, if there is to be any indeterminate inheritances, we require urgent ethical shifts in relationality and responsibility: a reckoning. While reconciliation proposes a determined outcome, reckoning opens up an indeterminate unknowable space inviting new relationalities. Indigenous knowledges, expertise, and land rights claims are precipitating a reckoning with (settler) colonial systems. The foundation of reckoning is Indigenous sovereignty; of lands and waters, governance, languages, educations, and cultures. As such, reckoning must both recognize and reject conceptual, theoretical, epistemological, and ontological moves to incorporate or otherwise claim Indigenous thought as its own. Whatever happens, reckoning must be oriented to destroying the Doctrine of Discovery and all of its legacies. Reckoning must be oriented to implementing *all* of the Truth and Reconciliation recommendations. Reckoning must be oriented to lands and waters; that which current reconciliation is oriented away from. As settler/colonial people, and as researchers in particular, we have much to do.

## Meanwhile, *Nuluujaat's* guardians step forward

Community meetings in the region hear Baffinalnd's proposal: doubling ore production, building a railway, and expanding the deep water port at Milne Inlet (Gignac, 2020). Many community members oppose expansion as narwhal, caribou, and walrus populations will be impacted (Gignac, 2021). Communities demand what the NCLA and IOL were meant to ensure: real decision-making power about how and when development happens on Inuit lands. Despite strong community opposition, the regional Inuit organization signs on to the expansion, prompting the mayors of the five surrounding hamlets and the chairs of local hunters and trappers associations to issue a joint letter criticizing the approval (Gignac, 2020).

In February 2021, the *Nuluujaat Land Guardians* block the Mary River Mine's airstrip in protest, insisting Baffinland cancel the expansion (Bell, 2021). Hundreds of Baffinland workers are stranded at the mine but show solidarity in an open letter of support for the protest, in the kind of "categories of people" allyship that Flanagan feared:

> This country has seen the consequences of entitlement and greed that have led to the destruction of the land for profit, and we are glad you are fighting for autonomy over your land. You've said that it is not the workers you are upset with, but the Baffinland executives, and we would like to say that our support is also not with our superiors in the company, but with you. On many occasions we've looked around at the massive piles of iron ore surrounded by miles of rusted snow, the colossal diesel tanks and the clouds of exhaust fumes that hang above the camp and thought, "What the hell are we doing here?".
>
> (CBC, 2021)

In the months following the *Nuluujaat Land Guardians'* protest, more Inuit communities, and environmental groups (WWF, 2022) join in the protest voices against Phase 2 of the mine and are heard. The regional Inuit organization withdraws support for the expansion (Bell, 2021), and in 2022, the federal Northern Affairs minister strikes the proposal down (Venn, 2022).

# Bibliography

ABC News. (2021). Canada Shocked by Unmarked Graves Found at Former Residential School Sites. *YouTube*. 7 July. https://www.youtube.com/watch?v=yb9R0wp7Dx0&ab_channel=ABCNews%28Australia%29

Agamben, G. (1998). *Homo Sacer: Sovereign Power and Bare Life*. Stanford University Press.

Amagoalik, J. (1976). *Presentation to the Mackenzie Valley Pipeline Inquiry*. Inuit Tapirisat of Canada.

Amagoalik, J. (1978). *Inuit Nunangat: The People's Land: A Struggle for Survival*. N.W.T. Inuit Land Claims Commission.

Anderson, W. (1995). Excremental Colonialism: Public Health and the Poetics of Pollution. *Critical Inquiry, 21*(3): 640–649.

APTN National News. (2019). *Reconciliation 'Isn't Just a Word,' Says Trudeau in First News Conference since Re-election*. 23 October. https://www.aptnnews.ca/national-news/reconciliation-isnt-just-a-word-says-trudeau-in-first-news-conference-since-re-election/

APTN National News. (2020). *Despite promise of reconciliation, Trudeau spent nearly $100M fighting First Nations in court during first years in power.* 18 December. https://www.aptnnews.ca/?s=Despite+promise+of+reconciliation%2C+Trudeau+spent+nearly+%24100M+fighting+First+Nations+in+court+during+first+years+in+power

Arboleda, M. (2020). *Planetary Mine: Territories of Extraction under Late Capitalism*. Verso Books.

Assembly of First Nations of Québec and Labrador. (2009). Prime Minister Harper Denies Colonialism in Canada at G20. *Cision*. 29 September. https://www.newswire.ca/news-releases/prime-minister-harper-denies-colonialism-in-canada-at-g20-538621372.html

Atamirano-Jiménez, I. (2014). *Indigenous Encounters with Neoliberalism: Place, Women and the Environment in Canada and Mexico*. University of Chicago Press.

Atleo, C. (2021). Between a Rock and a Hard Place: Canada's Carbon Economy and Indigenous Ambivalence. In W. Carroll (ed) *Regime of Obstruction: How Corporate Power Blocks Energy Democracy* (pp. 355–373). Edmonton: Athabasca Press.

Baffinland Iron Mines Limited. (1963). *Engineering Field Report No. 1 on the Mary River Iron Deposits.* Watts, Griffis and McOuat Limited.

Baffinland Iron Mines Limited. (1966). Feasibility Report and Cost Estimate: Baffinland Iron Project, Mary River, Baffin Island, N.W.T. Surveyer, Nenniger & Chênevert.

Baffinland Iron Mines Limited. (n.d.). *Mary River Mine.* Baffinland Website. https://baffinland.com/operation/mary-river-mine/.

Ballingall, A. (2020). 'Reconciliation Is Dead and We Will Shut Down Canada,' Wet'suwet'en Supporters Say. *Toronto Star.* 11 February. https://www.thestar.com/politics/federal/2020/02/11/reconciliation-is-dead-and-we-will-shut-down-canada-wetsuweten-supporters-say.html.

Barad, K. (2003). Posthumanist Performativity: Toward an Understanding of How Matter Comes to Matter. *Signs: Journal of Women in Culture and Society, 28*(3): 801–831. https://doi.org/10.1086/345321

Barad, K. (2007). *Meeting the Universe Halfway: Quantum Physics and the Entanglement of Matter and Meaning.* Duke University Press.

Barad, K. (2012). On Touching—The Inhuman That Therefore I Am. *Differences, 23*(3): 206–223. https://doi.org/10.1215/10407391-1892943

BC Gov News. (2019). Statement on Reconciliation Process between Province and Office of the Wet'suwet'en. 7 February. https://news.gov.bc.ca/releases/2019PREM0018-000195

Beckett, C. (2021). Beyond Remediation: Containing, Confronting and Caring for the Giant Mine Monster. *Environment and Planning E: Nature and Space, 4*(4): 1389–1412.

Bell, J. (2017). Nunavut Planning Commission Gets Started on Mary River Expansion. *Nunatsiaq News.* 6 September. https://nunatsiaq.com/stories/article/65674nunavut_planning_commission_gets_started_on_mary_river_expansion/.

Bell, J. (2021). Qikiqtani Inuit Association Won't Support Mary River Mine Expansion. *Nunatsiaq News.* 8 March. https://nunatsiaq.com/stories/article/qikiqtani-inuit-association-wont-support-mary-river-mine-expansion/

Bennett, J. (2010). *Vibrant Matter: A Political Ecology of Things.* Duke University Press.

Bernauer, W. (2019). Land Rights and Resource Conflicts in Nunavut. *Polar Geography, 42*(4): 253–266.

Blackadar, R.G. (1976). *The Geological Survey of Canada: Past Achievements and Future Goals: A Short History of the Geological Survey of Canada.* Ministry of Supply and Services Canada.

Blackadar, R.G. (n.d.). *The Day We Found Peary's Flag.* Blacklock's Reporter. https://www.blacklocks.ca/guest_commentary/the-day-we-found-pearys-flag/.

Blair, P.J. (2005). *The Non-Protection of Canadian Aboriginal Heritage (Burial Sites and Artifacts).* The Scow Institute. http://scow-archive.libraries.coop/library/documents/RPHeritageSites.pdf.

Borden, L.E. (1903–04). *Diary.* Public Archives of Canada, Ottawa (M.G. 30, C 52, vol. 2).

Braidotti, R. (2013). *The Posthuman.* Polity Press.

Braidotti, R. and Hlavajova, M. (2018). *Posthuman Glossary.* Bloomsbury Academic.

Brody, H. (2000). *The Other Side of Eden: Hungers, Farmers, and the Shaping of the World.* Douglas and McIntyre Publishing Group.

Boutet, J.S. (2014). Opening Ungava to Industry: A Decentring Approach to Indigenous History in Subarctic Québec, 1937–54. *Cultural Geographies, 21*(1): 79–97.

Burns, C., Orttung, R.W., Shaiman, M., Silinsky, L., and Zhang, E. (2021). Solid Waste Management in the Arctic. *Waste Management, 126*: 340–350. https://doi.org/10.1016/j.wasman.2021.03.021

Burton, M.I. (2017). *The Truth and Reconciliation Commission.* Ohio University Press.

Cameron, E. (2015). *Far off Metal River: Inuit lands, Settler Stories, and the Making of the Contemporary Arctic.* UBC Press.

Capozza, K.L. (2002). Ditched Drums and All. *Bulletin of the Atomic Scientists, 58*: 14–16.

Carleton, S. (2021). The Legacy of Oka in an Era of Supposed Reconciliation. *The Conversation.* 24 September. https://theconversation.com/the-legacy-of-oka-in-an-era-of-supposed-reconciliation-123150

Carroll, W. and Sapinski, J.P. (2018). *Organizing the 1%: How Corporate Power Works.* Fernwood Publishing.

Canadian Broadcasting Corporation (CBC) News. (2021a). *Stranded Baffinland Mine Workers Pen Open Letter to Protesters, Say They Support Inuit.* 11 February. https://www.cbc.ca/news/canada/north/baffinland-protestors-open-letter-1.5910951.

Canadian Broadcasting Corporation (CBC) News. (2021b). *Nunavut's MP Says Feeling 'Extremely Isolated' Spurred Decision Not to Run Again.* 21 June. https://www.cbc.ca/news/canada/north/nunavut-mp-mumilaaq-qaqqaq-interview-1.6065061

Canadian Broadcasting Corporation (CBC) News. (2022). *Beyond 94.* 8 June. https://www.cbc.ca/newsinteractives/beyond-94.

Canadian Press, The. (2023). Feasibility Study on Landfill Search for Manitoba Women's Remains Expected to be Done by March 31. https://www.cbc.ca/news/canada/manitoba/landfill-feasibility-study-remains-women-winnipeg-1.6717009

Chambraud, C. (2022). Pope Francis Acknowledges 'Genocide' of Indigenous Children in Canadian Schools Run by Catholic Congregations. *Le Monde*, 31 July. https://www.lemonde.fr/en/international/article/2022/07/31/pope-francis-acknowledges-genocide-of-indigenous-children-in-canadian-schools-run-by-catholic-congregations_5992018_4.html

Chin, F. and Pfeffer, A. (2021). Queen's University Response to False Indigenous Identity Claims 'Concerning,' Say Academics. *CBC News.* 15 June. https://www.cbc.ca/news/canada/ottawa/queens-university-open-letter-faculty-indigenous-ancestry-1.6065656

Chin, F. and Williams, N. (2021). Queen's University Defends Faculty, Staff against Allegations They're Falsely Claiming to be Indigenous. *CBC News.* 11 June. https://www.cbc.ca/news/canada/ottawa/queens-university-anonymous-report-indigenous-allegations-1.6063274

Clark, N. (2005). Ex-orbitant Globality. *Theory, Culture and Society, 22*(5): 165–185.

Clark, N. and Yusoff, K. (2017). Geosocial Formations and the Anthropocene. *Theory, Culture & Society, 34*(2–3): 3–23. https://doi.org/10.1177/0263276416688946

Cone, M. (2005). Rocket-Fuel Chemical Found in Breast Milk. *Los Angeles Times.* 23 February.

Coulthard, G.S. (2014). *Red Skin, White Masks: Rejecting the Colonial Politics of Recognition.* University of Minnesota Press.

Crone, J. (2022). Why Are We, Indigenous Women, Disposable Garbage? *ParrySound.* 15 December. https://www.parrysound.com/opinion-story/10809467-why-are-we-indigenous-women-disposable-garbage-asks-parry-sound-muskoka-columnist/

Cronon, W. (1996). The Trouble with Wilderness: Or, Getting Back to the Wrong Nature. *Environmental History, 1*(1): 7–28.

Cruikshank, J. (2012). Are Glaciers "Good to Think With"? Recognising Indigenous Environmental Knowledge. *Anthropological Forum, 22*(3): 239–250.

Dance, A., Monosky, M., Keeling, A. and Sandlos, J. (2022). Environmental Legacies: Mine Remediation Policy and Practice in Northern Canada. In C. Southcott,

F. Abele, D. Natcher and B. Parlee (eds) *Extractive Industry and the Sustainability of Canada's Arctic Communities* (pp. 196–230). McGill-Queen's University Press.

Danon-Schaffer, M. (2015). *Dumps, Landfills and Emerging Contaminants in the Canadian North.* RPIC Federal Contaminated Sites Regional Workshop, Edmonton, Alberta.

Deleuze, G. and Guattari, F. (1987). *A Thousand Plateaus: Capitalism and Schizophrenia.* University of Minnesota Press.

Deloria, V. (1973). *God Is Red: A Native View of Religion.* Dell.

Deloria, P. (1998). *Playing Indian.* Yale University Press.

Department of Health (2014). Bulletin: Questions and Answers Iqaluit Dump Fire - Air Quality. *Nunavut Department of Health*, released 18 July 2014.

Derrida, J. (1969). The Ends of Man. *Philosophy and Phenomenological Research, 30*(1): 31–57.

DIALOG. (nd). *St. Catherine's Milling Co. v. The Queen.* https://jurisprudence.reseau-dialog.ca/en/case/st-catherines-milling-co-v-the-queen/

Dillon, L. (2014). Race, Waste, and Space: Brownfield Redevelopment and Environmental Justice at the Hunters' Point Shipyard. *Antipode, 46*(5): 1205–1221.

Donaldson, S. and Kymlicka, W. (2011). *Zoopolis: A Political Theory of Animal Rights.* Oxford University Press.

Douglas, M. (1966/2007). *Purity and Danger: An Analysis of Concepts of Pollution and Taboo.* Routledge.

Ducharme, H.C. (2004). Here We Fight the Coldest War: Environmental Science and Feminist Autobiography of the DEW Line. [MA thesis, York University].

Duffy, R.Q. (1988). *The Road to Nunavut: The Progress of the Eastern Arctic Inuit Since the Second World War.* McGill-Queen's University Press.

Environmental Sciences Group. (1995). *Environmental Study of a Military Installation and Six Waste Disposal Sites at Iqaluit, NWT, vol. I: Site Analysis.* Indian and Northern Affairs Canada and Environment Canada.

Fanon, F. (1963). *The Wretched of the Earth.* Grove Press.

Farish, M. and Lackenbauer, P.W. (2009). High Modernism in the Arctic: Planning Frobisher Bay and Inuvik. *Journal of Historical Geography, 35*(3): 517–544.

First Peoples Group. (2022). *'Gii-ikidonaaniwan' 'It has been said': Queen's University Indigenous Identity Project Final Report.* https://www.queensu.ca/indigenous/sites/oiiwww/files/uploaded_files/FPG%20Queens%20Report%20Final%20July%207.pdf

Flaherty, C. (2021). Allegations of 'Playing' Indigenous. *Inside Higher Education.* 15 June. https://www.insidehighered.com/news/2021/06/15/allegations-playing-being-indigenous-queens-u

Forester, B. (2020). *Despite Promise of Reconciliation, Trudeau Spent Nearly $100M Fighting First Nations in Court during First Years in Power.* APTN. 18 December. https://www.aptnnews.ca/national-news/trudeau-spent-nearly-100m-fighting-first-nations-in-court-during-first-years-in-power/

Foucault, M. (1975/1977). *Discipline and Punish: The Birth of the Prison.* Pantheon Books.

Foucault, M. (1989 [1966]). *The Order of Things: An Archaeology of the Human Sciences.* Routledge.

Fuertes, D.C. (2010). The Haitian Revolution: Legacy and Actuality. *International Journal of Cuban Studies, 2*(3/4): 286–300.

Gignac, J. (2020). Review of Baffinland Mine Expansion in Nunavut Presses on, Despite Inuit Concerns. *The Narwhal*. 1 October. https://thenarwhal.ca/baffinland-mary-river-mine-expansion-inuit/.

Gignac, J. (2021). Massive Increase in Nunavut Mine Shipping Traffic Puts Narwhals at Risk: Study. *The Narwhal*. 19 February. https://thenarwhal.ca/massive-increase-in-nunavut-mine-shipping-traffic-puts-narwhals-at-risk-study/.

Gilmore, R. (2021). Trudeau Sorry for 'Incredibly Harmful' Residential Schools as Advocates Call for Accountability. *Global News*. 25 June. https://globalnews.ca/news/7980719/residential-schools-trudeau-apology-cowessess-751-unmarked-graves/

Godlewska, C. and Webber, J. (2007). The Calder Decision, Aboriginal Title, Treaties, and the Nisga'a. In H. Raven, J.H.A. Webber, and H. Foster (eds) *Let Right Be Done: Aboriginal Title, the Calder Case, and the Future of Indigenous Rights* (pp. 1–35). UBC Press.

Government of Canada. (1993). Agreement Between the Inuit of the Nunavut Settlement Area and Her Majesty the Queen in Right of Canada.

Government of Canada. (2010). *High Investment Potential in Canadian Northern Oil and Gas*. Indigenous and Northern Affairs Canada.

Government of Canada. (2014). *Canada's Northern Strategy*. Government of Canada.

Grek-Martin, J. (2009). Making Settler Space: George Dawson, the Geological Survey of Canada and the Colonization of the Canadian West in the Late 19th Century [PhD Dissertation, Queen's University]. https://qspace.library.queensu.ca/handle/1974/5142.

Griffiths, F., Huebert, R., and Lackenbauer, P. (2011). *Canada and the Changing Arctic*. Wilfred Laurier Press.

Habton, S. (2017). More Than a Bookstore, A Meeting Place with Itah Sadu. *The Henceforward Podcast*, Episode 15. http://www.thehenceforward.com/episodes/2017/10/2/episode-15-more-than-a-bookstore-a-meeting-place-featuring-itah-sadu

Haraway, D. (1988). Situated Knowledges: The Science Question in Feminism and the Privilege of Partial Perspective. *Feminist Studies*, *14*(3): 575–599.

Haraway, D. (2003). *The Companion Species Manifesto: Dogs, People and Significant Otherness*. University of Chicago Press.

Haraway, D.J. (2008). *When Species Meet*. University of Minnesota Press.

Heaps, L. (1978). *Operation Morning Light: Terror in Our Skies*. Paddington Press.

Henderson, A. (2007). *Nunavut: Rethinking Political Culture*. UBC Press.

Henri, D. (2012). Managing Nature, Producing Cultures: Inuit Participation, Science and Policy in Wildlife Governance in the Nunavut Territory, Canada. [Ph.D. thesis, Oxford University].

Hird, M.J. (2009). *The Origins of Sociable Life: Evolution After Science Studies*. Palgrave Press.

Hird, M.J. (2012). Knowing Waste: Towards an Inhuman Epistemology. *Social Epistemology*, *26*(3–4): 453–469.

Hird, M.J. (2015). In/human Waste Environments. *GLQ: A Journal of Lesbian and Gay Studies*. Special issue on Queer Inhumanisms, *21*(2–3): 213–215.

Hird, M.J. (2016a). The DEW Line and Canada's Arctic Waste: Legacy and Futurity. *The Northern Review*, *42*: 23–45.

Hird, M.J. (2016b). The Phenomenon of Waste-World-Making. *Rhizomes: Cultural Studies in Emerging Knowledge*, 30.

Hird, M.J. and Zahara, A. (2017). The Arctic Wastes. In R. Grusin (ed) *Anthropocene Feminism* (pp. 121–146). University of Minnesota Press.

Hird, M.J. (2021). *Canada's Waste Flows*. McGill-Queen's University Press.

Hird, M.J. (2022). *A Public Sociology of Waste*. Bristol University Press.

Holy Press Office (2023). Joint Statement of the Dicasteries for Culture and Education and for Promoting Integral Human Development on the "Doctrine of Discovery". https://press.vatican.va/content/salastampa/en/bollettino/pubblico/2023/03/30/230330b.html Accessed 15 May 2023.

Hoogeveen, D. (2015). Sub-surface Property, Free-entry Mineral Staking and Settler Colonialism in Canada. *Antipode*, *47*(1): 121–138. https://doi-org.proxy.queensu.ca/10.1111/anti.12095

Howard-Wagner, D., Bargh, M. and Atamirano-Jiménez, I. (2018). *The Neoliberal State, Recognition and Indigenous Rights: New Paternalism and New Imaginings*. Australian National University Press.

Hunt, S. (2014). Ontologies of Indigeneity: The Politics of Embodying a Concept. *Cultural Geographies*, *21*(1): 27–32.

Huseman, J. and Short, D. (2012). "A Slow Industrial Genocide": Oil Sands and the Indigenous Peoples of Northern Alberta. *International Journal of Human Rights*, *16*(1): 216–237.

Indian Residential Schools Settlement Agreement. (2006). *Schedule "N"*. https://www.residentialschoolsettlement.ca/schedule_n.pdf.

Irigaray, L. (1974). *Speculum of the Other Woman*. Trans. 1985 by Gillian C. Gill. Cornell University Press.

Irwin, R. (2018). *Aboriginal Title*. The Canadian Encyclopedia. https://www.thecanadianencyclopedia.ca/en/article/aboriginal-title

Isuma.tv. (n.d.). *Who Is Baffinland?* Isuma.tv. http://www.isuma.tv/ashleigh-gaul/who-is-baffinland.

Jenness, D. (1959). *The People of the Twilight*. University of Chicago Press.

Johnson, J.T., Howitt, R., Cajete, G., Berkes, F., Pualani Louis, R. and Kliske, A. (2016). Weaving Indigenous and Sustainability Sciences to Diversify our Methods. *Sustainability Science*, *11*: 1–11.

Kafarowski, J. (2004). Gender, Culture, and Contaminants in the North. *Signs*, *34*(3): 494–499.

Kalinovich, I., Rutter, A., Poland, J.S., Cairns, G. and Rowe, R.K. (2008). Remediation of PCB Contaminated Soils in the Canadian Arctic: excavation and Surface PRB Technology. *Science of the Total Environment*, *407*(1): 53–66.

Kennedy, D. (2022). 'Biggest fake news story in Canada': Kamloops Mass Grave Debunked by Academics. *New York Post*. 27 May. https://nypost.com/2022/05/27/kamloops-mass-grave-debunked-biggest-fake-news-in-canada/

Korzybski, A (1958 [1931]). *Science and Sanity: An Introduction to Non-Aristotelian Systems and General Semantics*. Institute of General Semantics.

Kristeva, J. (1982). *Powers of Horror: An Essay on Abjection*. Trans. L. Roudiez. Columbia University Press.

Krupar, S. (2013). *Hot Spotter's Report: Military Fables of Toxic Waste*. University of Minnesota Press.

Kuyek, J. (2019). *Unearthing Justice: How to Protect Your Community from the Mining Industry*. Between the Lines.

Lackenbauer, P. and Farish, M. (2007). The Cold War on Canadian Soil: Militarizing a Northern Environment. *Environmental History*, *12*(4): 920–950.

Lackenbauer, P. and Shackleton, R. (2012). *When the Skies Rained Boxes: The Air Force and the Qikiqtani Inuit, 1941–64*. Working Papers on Arctic Security No. 4. Toronto: Walter and Duncan Gordon Foundation and ArcticNet Arctic Security Projects.

la paperson. (2017). *A Third University Is Possible*. University of Minnesota Press.

Lathers, M. (2006). Towards and Excremental Posthumanism: Primatology, Women, and Waste. *Society and Animals, 14*(4): 417–436.

Latour, B. (2017). *Facing Gaia. Eight Lectures on the New Climatic Regime*. Oxford: Polity Press.

Leo, G. (2022). New University of Sask. Commissioned Report Tackles 'Poison' of Indigenous Identity Fraud. *CNC News*. https://www.cbc.ca/news/canada/saskatchewan/new-independent-university-report-tackles-indigenous-identity-1.6639470

Lepawsky, J. (2018). *Reassembling Rubbish: Worlding Electronic Waste*. MIT Press.

Liberal Party of Canada. (2015). *Liberals Call for Full Implementation of Truth and Reconciliation Commission Recommendations*. 2 June. https://liberal.ca/liberals-call-for-full-implementation-of-truth-and-reconciliation-commission-recommendations/

Liboiron, M. (2021). *Pollution is Colonialism*. Duke University Press.

Liboiron, M. and Lepawsky, J. (2022). *Discard Studies: Wasting, Systems, and Power*. MIT Press.

Locke, J. (1869/2011). *Second Treatise of Government*. Edited by H. Laski. CreateSpace independent Publishing Platform.

Loveless, N. (2019). *How to Make Art at the End of the World: A Manifesto for Research-Creation*. Duke University Press.

Low, A.P. (1906). *The Cruise of the Neptune, the Dominion Government Expedition to Hudson Bay and the Arctic Islands on Board the D.G.S. Neptune, 1903–1904*. Government Printing Bureau.

Lowman, E.B. and Barker, A.J. (2015). *Settler: Identity and Colonialism in 21st Century Canada*. Fernwood Publishing.

Lukacs, M. (2019). *The Trudeau Formula: Seduction and Betrayal in an Age of Discontent*. Black Rose Books.

Lukas, M. (2022). Reconciliation: The False Promise of Trudeau's Sunny Ways. *The Walrus*, 24 March. https://thewalrus.ca/the-false-promise-of-trudeaus-sunny-ways/

MacDonald, F. (2011). Indigenous Peoples and Neoliberal 'Privatization' in Canada: Opportunities, Cautions and Constraints. *Canadian Journal of Political Science, 44*(2): 257–273.

Maniates, M. (2001). Plant a Tree, Buy a Bike, Save the World? In: T. Princen, M. Maniates and K. Conca (eds) *Confronting Consumption* (pp. 43–66). MIT Press.

Manuel, G. and Posluns, M. (1974). *The Fourth World: An Indian Reality*. University of Minnesota Press.

Marshall, M., Marshall, A. and Bartlett, C. (2012). Two-Eyed Seeing and Other Lessons Learned within a Co-learning Journey of Bringing Together Indigenous and Mainstream Knowledges and Ways of Knowing. *Journal of Environmental Studies and Sciences, Springer;Association of Environmental Studies and Sciences, 2*(4): 331–340.

Martineau, J., and Ritskes, E.J. (2014). Fugitive Indigeneity: Reclaiming the Terrain of Decolonial Struggle through Indigenous art. *Decolonization: Indigeneity, Education & Society, 3*(1): I–XII.

Martin, J., Roy, E., Diemont, S. and Ferguson, B. (2010). Traditional Ecological Knowledge (TEK): Ideas, Inspiration, and Designs for Ecological Engineering. *Ecological Engineering, 36*: 839–849.

May, H. (2022). Airdrie-Cochrane MLA Peter Guthrie Named Minister of Energy. *Cochrane Today*. 21 October.

McCreary, T. and Milligan, R. (2014). Pipelines, Permits, and Protests: Carrier Sekani Encounters with the Enbridge Northern Gateway Project. *Cultural Geographies, 21*(1): 115–129.

McGregor, D., Whitaker, S. and Sritharan, M. (2020). Indigenous Environmental Justice and Sustainability. *Current Opinions in Environmental Sustainability, 43*: 35–40.

McIvor, B. (2020). Reconciliation at the End of a Gun: The Wet'suwet'en and the RCMP. *First People's Law*. 7 February. https://www.firstpeopleslaw.com/public-education/blog/reconciliation-at-the-end-of-a-gun-the-wetsuweten-and-the-rcmp

McIvor, B. (2021). *Standoff: Why Reconciliation Fails Indigenous People and How to Fix It*. Nightwood Editions.

McNeil, K. (1997). Aboriginal Title and Aboriginal Rights: What's the Connection? *Alberta Law Review, 36*(1): 117–148.

McPherson, R. (2003). *New Owners in Their Own Land: Minerals and Inuit Land Claims*. University of Calgary Press.

Merritt, J. (1989). *Nunavut: Political Choices and Manifest Destiny*. Canadian Arctic Resources Committee.

Newcomb, S.T. (2008). *Pagans in the Promised Land: Decoding the Doctrine of Christian Discovery*. Fulcrum Publisher.

Nunatsiaq News. (2016). Nunavut Regulator Hands Mary River an Unflattering Report Card. *Nunatsiaq News*. 11 November. https://nunatsiaq.com/stories/article/65674nunavut_regulator_hands_mary_river_an_unflattering_report_card

Nunatsiaq News. (2017). Arbitration Hearing on QIA-Baffinland Royalties Dispute Starts April 18. *Nunatsiaq News*. 18 April. https://nunatsiaq.com/stories/article/65674arbitration_hearing_on_qia-baffinland_financial_dispute_starts_april_1 /.

Nunavut Constitutional Forum. (1985). *Building Nunavut: Today and Tomorrow: The Nunavut Constitutional Proposal*. Nunavut Constitutional Forum.

Nunavut Implementation Commission. (1995). Footprints in New Snow: A Comprehensive Report from the Nunavut Implementation Commission to the Department of Indian Affairs and Northern Development, Government of the Northwest Territories and Nunavut Tunngavik Incorporated Concerning the Establishment of the Nunavut Government. Nunavut Implementation Commission.

Nunavut Tunngavik Inc. (NTI). (n.d.). *Explore the Potential of Inuit Owned Lands*. https://www.tunngavik.com/files/2011/03/lands_brochure.pdf.

Nunn, N. (2018). Toxic Encounters, Settler Logics of Elimination, and the Future of a Continent. *Antipode, 50*(5): 1–19.

Obbard, R.W., Sadri, S., Wong, Y.Q., Khitun, A., Baker, I. and Thompson, R. (2014). Global Warming Releases Microplastic Legacy Frozen in Arctic Sea Ice. *Earth's Future, 2*(6): 315–320.

Oneida Nation. (nd). *The Haudenosaunee Creation Story*. https://www.oneidaindiannation.com/the-haudenosaunee-creation-story/.

Orphan Well Association. (2023). Orphan Inventory. https://www.orphanwell.ca/about/orphan-inventory/

Paine, R., ed. (1977). *The White Arctic: Anthropological Essays on Tutelage and Ethnicity*. Memorial University of Newfoundland.

Pasternak, S. (2014). How Capitalism Will Save Colonialism: The Privatization of Reserve Lands in Canada. *Antipode, 47*(1): 179–196. https://doi.org/10.1111/anti.12094

Patterson, D. (2023) Mixed Feelings from Sask. Indigenous People after Catholic Church Repudiates Doctrine of Discovery. *CBC News Saskatchewan*, https://www.cbc.ca/news/canada/saskatoon/mixed-feelings-indigenous-people-repudiation-doctrine-of-discovery-1.6796852 Accessed 15 May 2023.

Perić, S. (2015). Darwin's North: Military Adaptation and the Birth of Counterinsurgency in the Land of Oil and Ice. Paper presented at the *American Anthropological Association*, 2015 Annual Meeting, 21 November.

Pizzolato, L., Howell, S., Derksen, C., Dawson, J. and Copland, L. (2014). Changing Sea Ice Conditions and Marine Transportation Activity in Canadian Arctic Waters Between 1990 and 2012. *Climate Change*, *123*(1): 161–173.

Poland, J.S., Mitchell, S. and Rutter, A. (2001). Remediation of Fomer Military Bases in the Canadian Arctic. *Cold Regions Science and Technology*, *32*(2–3): 93–105.

Predko, H. (2022). Relationship to the Land (Use Planning Provisions): Mapping the Limitations of the Settler Imagination in an Arctic Anthropocene. [MES Thesis, Queen's University]. https://qspace.library.queensu.ca/handle/1974/30034.

Preston, J. (2013). Neoliberal Settler Colonialism, Canada and the Tar Sands. *Race and Class, 55*(2): 42–59.

Price, J. (2007). Tukisivallialiqtakka: The Things I Have Now Begun to Understand: Inuit Governance, Nunavut and the Kitchen Consultation Model. [MA Thesis, University of New Brunswick].

Qikiqtani Inuit Association. (2010). *Qikiqtami Truth Commission Final Report: Achieving Saimaqtigiiniq*. Qikiqtani Inuit Association.

Qikiqtani Inuit Association. (2013). *Paliisikkut: Policing in Qikiqtaaluk*. Inhabit Media. https://www.qtcommission.ca/sites/default/files/public/thematic_reports/thematic_reports_english_paliisikkut.pdf.

Qikiqtani Inuit Association (QIA). (n.d.). *Mary River Project*. QIA.ca. https://www.qia.ca/about-us/departments/major-projects/what-is-the-mary-river-project/

Queen's University. (n.d.). *Office of Indigenous Initiatives*. https://www.queensu.ca/indigenous/

Queen's University. (2022). *Queen's Releases Report Following Dialogues on Indigeneity*. Queen's Gazette. https://www.queensu.ca/gazette/stories/queen-s-releases-report-following-dialogues-indigeneity.

Regan, P. (2010). *Unsettling the Settler Within Indian Residential Schools, Truth Telling, and Reconciliation in Canada*. UBC Press.

Reid, J. (2010). The Doctrine of Discovery and Canadian Law. *The Canadian Journal of Native Studies*, *2*(2010): 335–359.

Reid, A.J., Eckert, L.E., Lane, J-F., et al. (2021). "Two-Eyed Seeing": An Indigenous Framework to Transform Fisheries Research and Management. *Fish Fish, 22*: 243–261.

Ridgen, M. (2021). Pretendians and What to Do with People Who Falsely Say They're Indigenous Put InFocus. *APTN News*. https://www.aptnnews.ca/infocus/pretendians-and-what-to-do-with-people-who-falsely-say-theyre-indigenous-put-infocus/.

Ross, W.G. (1976). Canadian Sovereignty in the Arctic: The "Neptune" Expedition of 1903–04. *Arctic*, *29*(2): 87–104. http://www.jstor.org/stable/40509260

Rowe, R.K. (2012). Design and Construction of Barrier Systems to Minimize Environmental Impacts Due to Municipal Solid Waste Leachate and Gas. Third Indian Geotechnical Society, Ferroco Terzaghi Oration. *Indian Geotech Journal*, *42*(4): 223–256.

Rushmore, S. (2020). "We Are All Related: A Conversation with Stan Rushworth". Spiritual Ecology and Action | Episode 34, Earthfire Radio, Earthfire Institute, https://earthfireinstitute.org/podcads/we-are-all-related-a-conversation-with-stan-rushworth/.

Sandlos, J. and Keeling, A. (2012). Claiming the New North: Development and Colonialism at the Pine Point Mine, Northwest Territories, Canada. *Environment and History*, *18*(1): 5–34.

Saul, J. (2008). *A Fair Country: Telling Truths about Canada*. Penguin Canada.

Scace, R. (1975). *Exploration, Settlement and Land Use Activities in Northern Canada: A Historical Review*. Inuit Tapirisat of Canada.

Scanlan, J. (2005). *On Garbage*. Reaktion Books.

Sefa Dei, G.J. (2002). Rethinking the Role of Indigenous Knowledges in the Academy. NALL Working Paper. Ontario Inst. for Studies in Education, Toronto. *New Approaches to Lifelong Learning*. https://files.eric.ed.gov/fulltext/ED479137.pdf.

Simpson, L.R. (2004). Anticolonial Strategies for the Recovery and Maintenance of Indigenous Knowledge. *American Indian Quarterly, 28*(3/4): 373–384.

Sinclair, K. (2017). *Iron Ore and Well-Being: Inuit Engagements with Mining* [Doctoral dissertation, McGill University]. Library and Archives Canada. https://library-archives.canada.ca/eng/services/services-libraries/theses/Pages/item.aspx?idNumber=1000103221.

Singer, P. (1975). *Animal Liberation*. HarperCollins.

Smith, L.T. (2021). *Decolonizing Methodologies: Research and Indigenous Peoples*. Zed Books.

Southcott, C. (2012). Can Resource Development Make Arctic Communities Sustainable? *Northern Public Affairs (spring)*: 48–49.

Spivak, G. (1988). Can the Subaltern Speak? In C. Nelson and L. Grossberg (eds) *Marxism and the Interpretation of Culture* (pp. 271–313). Macmillan.

Stephenson, M. and Gilmore, R. (2021). Trudeau Spends 1st Truth and Reconciliation Day in Tofino on Vacation, Contradicting Itinerary. *Global News*. 30 September. https://globalnews.ca/news/8234246/trudeau-vacation-indigenous-tofino-truth-and-reconciliation/.

Sundberg, J. (2014). Decolonizing Posthumanist Geographies. *Cultural Geographies, 21*(1): 33–47. https://doi.org/10.1177/1474474013486067

Tagaq, T. [@tagaq] (2022). *Get Me the Native Trauma Donut* [Tweet]. Twitter. https://twitter.com/tagaq/status/1575859358290018304.

Taylor, S. (2022). Canada Agreed to 'Forever Discharge' Catholic Entities from Raising $25M for Residential School Survivors. *CBC News*. 20 August. https://www.cbc.ca/news/politics/canada-deal-catholic-church-fundraising-1.6557533

Thomassin-Lacroix, E. (2015). *Site Remediation of the Former DEW Line Site at FOX-3 Dewar Lakes, Nunavut*. RPIC Federal Contaminated Sites Regional Workshop, Edmonton, Alberta.

Tlostanova, M.V. (2015). Can the Post-Soviet Think? On Coloniality of Knowledge, External Imperial and Double Colonial Difference. *Intersections. East European Journal of Society and Politics, 1*(2): 38–58.

Todd, Z. (2015). Indigenizing the Anthropocene. In H. Davis and E. Turpin (eds) *Art in the Anthropocene: Encounters Among Aesthetics, Politics, Environment and Epistemology* (pp. 241–254). Open Humanities Press.

Todd, Z. (2016). An Indigenous Feminist's Take on the Ontological Turn: 'Ontology' Is Just Another Word for Colonialism. *Journal of Historical Sociology, 29*(1): 4–22. https://doi.org/10.1111/johs.12124

ToDoCanada. (2022). *Tim Hortons' Orange-Sprinkled Fundraising Donut is Back in Support of Indigenous Charities.* 26 September. https://www.todocanada.ca/get-tim-hortons-orange-sprinkled-donut-2022/

The Truth and Reconciliation Commission of Canada (2015). *Canada's Residential Schools: Missing Children and Unmarked Burials.* McGill-Queen's University Press.

Tsing, A.L., Deger, J., Saxena, A.K. and Zhou, F. (2021). *Introduction to Feral Atlas.* The Feral Atlas. https://feralatlas.supdigital.org/

Tuck, E. and Yang, K.W. (2012). Decolonization Is Not a Metaphor. *Decolonization: Indigeneity, Education & Society*, *1*(1): 1–40.

Turner, L. (2023). Ontario Mines Minister says Ring of Fire Could Be Worth $1 Trillion, a Figure Critics Call Exaggerated. *CBC News*, 17 March. https://www.cbc.ca/news/canada/thunder-bay/ring-of-fire-trillion-dollar-claim-1.6778551

Union of Ontario Indians. (2013). *An Overview of the Indian Residential School System.* https://www.anishinabek.ca/wp-content/uploads/2016/07/An-Overview-of-the-IRS-System-Booklet.pdf

*Up Here: Life in Canada's Far North Magazine.* (2014). July/August.

van Wyck, P. (2010). *The Highway of the Atom.* McGill-Queen's University Press.

Varga, P. (2014). City Can't Douse Iqaluit's Latest Massive Dump Fire. *Nunatsiaq News.* 21 May.

Venn, D. (2022). Vandal Rejects Baffinland's Phase 2 Expansion; Company Expected to Release Statement Thursday. *Nunatsiaq News.* 16 November. https://nunatsiaq.com/stories/article/vandal-rejects-baffinlands-phase-2-expansion-agrees-with-review-board/.

Veracini, L. (2010). *Settler Colonialism.* Palgrave Macmillan.

Veracini, L. (2011). Introducing Settler Colonial Studies. *Settler Colonial Studies*, *1*(1): 1–12.

Wachowich, N. (1994). Women's Traditional Governance Research Project, Inuit Women in Pond Inlet Speak About Power. Edmonton: Royal Commission on Indigenous Peoples.

Wapner, P. (1996). Toward a Meaningful Ecological Politics. *Tikkun*, *11*(3): 21–22.

Watts, V. (2013). Indigenous Place-Thought and Agency Amongst Humans and Non-Humans (First Woman and Sky Woman Go On a European World Tour!). *Decolonization: Indigeneity, Education & Society*, *2*(1): 20–34.

Wente, Jesse (2021). *Unreconciled: Family, Truth, and Indigenous Resistance.* Penguin Random House.

Whyte, K. (2017). Indigenous Climate Change Studies: Indigenizing Futures, Decolonizing the Anthropocene. *English Language Notes*, *55*(1): 153–162.

Wilson, S. (2008). *Research Is Ceremony: Indigenous Research Methods.* Fernwood Publishing.

Wilson-Raybould, J. (2023). *True Reconciliation: How to Be a Force for Change.* McClelland & Stewart.

Wong, C., Ballegoyen, K., Ignace, L., Johnson, M.J., and Swanson, H. (2020). Towards Reconciliation: 10 Calls to Action to Natural Scientists Working in Canada. *FACETS*, 5: 769–783.

Wright, C. and Nyberg, D. (2015). *Climate Change, Capitalism, and Corporations.* Cambridge University Press.

WWF. (2022). *Government of Canada Must Respect Inuit Concerns, Reject Mary River Mine Expansion.* https://wwf.ca/media-releases/government-canada-baffinland-expansion/.

Yellowhead Institute. (2022). *Calls to Action Accountability: A 2022 Status Update on Reconciliation.*   https://yellowheadinstitute.org/wp-content/uploads/2022/12/TRC-Report-12.15.2022-Yellowhead-Institute-min.pdf.

Yerxa, J.R. (2012). Refuse to Live Quietly! Indigenous Nationhood Movement [blog]. In E. Battell Lowman and A.J. Barker (eds) *Settler: Identity and Colonialism in 21st Century Canada* (p. 22). Fernwood Publishing.

Yusoff, K. (2013). Geologic Life: Prehistory, Climate, Futures in the Anthropocene. *Environment and Planning D: Society and Space, 31*(5): 779–795.

Yusoff, K. (2017). Geosocial Strata. *Theory, Culture & Society, 34*(2–3): 105–127.

Yusoff, K. (2018). *A Billion Black Anthropocenes or None.* University of Minnesota Press.

Yusoff, K. (2021). The Inhumanities. *Annals of the American Association of Geographers, 111*(3): 663–676. https://doi.org/10.1080/24694452.2020.1814688

Zaslow, M. (1975). *Reading the Rocks: The Story of the Geological Survey of Canada, 1842–1972.* Macmillan Company of Canada, Department of Energy, Mines and Resources.

Zembylas, M. (2018). The Entanglement of Decolonial and Posthuman Perspectives: Tensions and Implications for Curriculum and Pedagogy in Higher Education. *Parallax, 24*(3): 254–267.

# Index

For Product Safety Concerns and Information please contact our EU
representative GPSR@taylorandfrancis.com
Taylor & Francis Verlag GmbH, Kaufingerstraße 24, 80331 München, Germany

www.ingramcontent.com/pod-product-compliance
Lightning Source LLC
Chambersburg PA
CBHW071057280326
41928CB00050B/2544